The Abbot's Shoes

The Abbot's Shoes

Seeking a Contemplative Life

Peter Robertson

Revival Streams
Auckland, New Zealand

© Peter Robertson 2015, 2018

Peter Robertson asserts his moral right to be identified as the author of this work.

All rights reserved. No part of this publication may be produced or transmitted in any form or by any means, electronic or mechanical, including photocopying, recording or information storage and retrieval systems, without permission in writing from the copyright holder.

A catalogue record for this book is available from the National Library of New Zealand.

Published by Revival Streams, Auckland, New Zealand

www.revivalstreams.co.nz

Cover design: www.intuitcreative.net

Unless otherwise stated, all Scripture taken from the HOLY BIBLE, NEW INTERNATIONAL VERSION. Copyright 1973, 1978, 1984 by International Bible Society. Used by permission of Zondervan. All rights reserved.

"Prayer, as our greatest work breeds in us the flair for the greatest work of God." — Peter T. Forsyth, *The Soul of Prayer*

"In prayer we drink the dregs of our poverty, professing the richness and grandeur of someone else: God." — Johannes B. Metz, *Poverty of Spirit*

"Read it as best you can, for I am writing it as best I can, and, if it is too bad, burn it." — Teresa of Avila, *Way of Perfection*

Contents

	Introduction	1
1.	The Abbot's Shoes	*3*
2.	Now or Never	*9*
3.	Utter Simplicity	*15*
4.	Father Louis	*21*
5.	Bare Bones	*27*
6.	Fading Away	*33*
7.	Sea Change	*39*
8.	Altogether Different	*45*
9.	False Start	*49*
10.	Hidden Power	*57*

11.	Not Alone	*63*
12.	A Thorny Issue	*69*
13.	Real World	*75*
14.	At Play	*81*
15.	An Apprentice	*85*
16.	Life Together	*91*
17.	Just Thinking	*97*
18.	The Hermit	*103*
19.	For Everyone	*109*
20.	Joy Unspeakable	*115*
21.	Pear Seeds	*121*
22.	Pathways	*125*
23.	Prophet's Death	*131*
24.	The Tangi	*137*
25.	Radical Politics	*143*
26.	No Ladders	*149*
27.	The Fairer	*155*
28.	Shadows	*161*

29.	Adrift	*167*
30.	Runaway	*173*
31.	'Tis Mystery	*179*
32.	Great Preoccupation	*185*
33.	The Smallest	*191*
	Glossary	*199*
	About the Author	*201*

Introduction

Our Lady of the Southern Star Abbey in the Hawke's Bay of New Zealand belongs to the Cistercian Order, a "community" of contemplative monasteries scattered all around the world. Their history began in a reformation of Benedictine monasticism in France during the 12th century. There arose at that time amongst these white-cowled monks "one of the greatest spiritual masters of all times", Bernard of Clairvaux. During his lifetime, he oversaw the "planting" of 65 new Cistercian communities. Today these men and women who "live to pray" and whose work is prayer are often known as Trappists, as the result of a further reformation of their movement during the 17th century at La Trappe in France.

1

The Abbot's Shoes

Autumn always finds me restless. I am beset with the feeling that I ought to be getting ready to go somewhere else. Perhaps it is some ancient memory of migration. Maybe an impulse inherited from agricultural ancestors, who knew when to obey nature's signs and move from summer to winter pastures.

In the autumn of 1972, I was 22 years old and living with everything "up in the air", anyway. I recall feeling hopefully restless. At the time my "home" was what appeared to have been a shoemaker's workshop, which was part of a long timber and iron shed, used mainly for storing machinery and onions. It sat buried in an orchard towards the rear of the enclosure of Our Lady of the Southern Star Abbey on Kopua Road in central Hawke's Bay.

My days were then framed by the prayers of the Liturgy of the Hours and clothed with farm labour. I revelled in both. For the most part I worked with the sub-Prior, Father Basil, who looked after the monastery's sheep farm. One afternoon he told me that he was "away to Wellington" the next morning, and the Abbot had said I was to travel with him. I suppose that this was some kind of "mental health" break; a day off from the "isolation" and "intensity" of a contemplative community that could trace its roots back a thousand years to France. I think I felt rather ambivalent about the expedition. I'd waited for three years to "escape" my world of newspaper deadlines, pub culture and selfish relationships. I was in no hurry to return.

That evening there came a knock on the door of my shed, and there in all his abbatial splendour stood Father Joseph ... "the Boss". Described by others as "a tall, big-boned and impressive man ... (with an) aura of calm authority"[1], here was some-

---

[1]. NZ Herald, 18 November 1986

The Abbot's Shoes

one not to be trifled with. I do not think we had exchanged many words up until that moment. He was in a very real sense of the word a "prince" of the Church, whereas I was a scruffy, half-baked Protestant who wanted to be a monk. Father Joseph held in one hand a pair of extra-large, black shoes; his shoes ... solid, well worn, well polished. "Ye'll be needing these, Brother ... for your trip tomorrow." The Abbot disappeared quite quickly back along the orchard path, with my mumbled, slightly baffled thanks bouncing off his black-scapulared back. I can only assume that a higher power had decided that neither my sandals nor my filthy work boots were suitable footwear for a day-trip to New Zealand's capital city.

My "big" day out was remarkable for two things ... a conversation and discomfort. With time to kill in the Big Smoke, I remembered that a former colleague was working as a journalist for Radio New Zealand. Jack was a good deal older than me, but I had grown to respect and admire him. He was an old-style, hardworking reporter and a quietly devout Catholic. He was surprised when I turned up at his desk, and amazed to hear about my situation. He had last observed me, probably drunk, and doing a whole lot more talking than serious work. Jack listened silently and intently to the description of my new life of prayer that was work, and work that was prayer. When I paused my monologue to draw breath, he quietly said, "I do really envy you. I wish I had done that. Chaos and decay … chaos and decay." Jack's lunchtime reverie was not a moralistic, puritanical rant. He was a mellow and tolerant Christian, a seasoned newspaperman not easily startled by vice and corruption. His statement affected me profoundly because he was touching something of the depths of existence; that mankind so carefully and beautifully fashioned for Heaven could degenerate and slide so easily into Hell.

As for the discomfort? Well, the Abbot's shoes had tacks sticking up through their soles. Walking was painful. To this day Father Joseph's shoes are a great mystery to me. Was the monastery's shoemaker guilty of poor workmanship and did "the Boss" out of Christian charity decide not to upbraid a brother? Or had he, as an old-school "son" of the ascetical Bernard of Clairvaux, chosen to walk in His Saviour's footsteps? "If anyone would come after me, he must deny himself and take up his cross and follow me."[2] I don't know. I do know however that on that day Father Joseph wore his slippers to work to pray, so his littlest Brother could wander the streets of Wellington suitably shod.

2. Matthew 16.24

2

Now or Never

In 1971, my transition within 24 hours from inner city living to the desolate, rural railway station at Takapau was stunning ... and frightening. As my railcar cracked off into the distance and towards Gisborne, a terrible sensation of emptiness swirled around me, triggering a feeling not unlike panic. As advised, I crossed the village's main street to its garage and petrol station, which also doubled as the district's taxi service. There appeared to be nothing of any note at the end of the driveway up to the monastery, just a couple of modest wooden buildings. Some had been used in another place to shelter wartime refugee children.

The Abbot's Shoes

Knowing virtually nothing about the monastic life, my first thoughts were that I had arrived too late, that the place was a ghost ship and the whole crew had vanished. Within a day or so, I had learnt that the community lived together, "hidden" in the enclosure behind the guest house, church and chapter room. They gathered together six times through each day and night to sing the Psalms and pray their Offices.

During my regulation week's retreat, I was unusually isolated and left to my own devices. A renowned, Benedictine scholar and author was visiting. Dom Jean Leclercq[1] impressed me as a speaker and a consumer of hot water. Morning and night this good monk beat me to the entire contents of the guest house's hot-water cylinder. Eventually, I got crafty and started taking a shower in the middle of the day. Dom Jean took all his meals in the guest house and simultaneously hosted conversations with some of the abbey's seniors. This meant I ate alone in my room, sat alone at the back of the church, and walked alone around the monastery's pathways and fields.

---

1. Dom Jean Leclercq (1911–93) Luxembourg. His voluminous writings about Bernard of Clairvaux were considered the "most comprehensive ever undertaken".

But the community itself most graciously broke my enforced solitude by inviting me into their chapter room to listen to their visitor's talks. Marvellous! Here I was, sitting in the same room and hearing from someone who had been a personal friend of my contemplative hero, Thomas Merton. My random reading of Merton's best-selling autobiography, *The Seven Storey Mountain*[2], in November 1968 (just before the author's untimely death) had sparked a passion for the monastic life and inspired my journey to Takapau.

Nevertheless I continued to feel lonely and haunted by the sense of distance from home (more than 12 hours by train), and in the evenings had to battle sudden urges to "make a run" for the railway station. I'm glad I didn't.

By my final evening at the abbey, the VIP was on his way and I was admitted (still alone) to take my evening meal in the guest house dining room. A relieving guest-master made his appearance. The gentle Father Basil[3] sat with me during my meal, plying me with discreet enquiries and uncomplainingly and patiently answering my naïve and some-

---

2. "The Seven Storey Mountain" (Harcourt Brace & Co., NY 1948)
3. Father Basil (from County Tipperary, Ireland) founded the monastery in 1954. He was then 35 years old.

times inane questions. Later we sat for a while on a bench on the veranda with its view east over rolling farmland and hills. Then out of the blue I was asked, "Why are you here?" At this point everything went into slow motion, because I had come with a very particular question that I doubted could ever be answered positively. But I thought, "This is the only chance you'll ever have to ask. It's now or never."

"Father," I replied, "I'm not a Catholic ... or anything much really. But I would like to come and live here."

Realistically I had expected at best a polite but firm demur, at worst a list of all the reasons why such a proposal was outlandish. Certainly the lull in our conversation was unpromisingly lengthy, but the reply was stunning. "Well ... I don't really see any great problem with that. Why don't you go back to Auckland and give it some more thought. If you're still of the same mind, then write to me, and I'll see what's to be done."

I can still see the blue aerogramme with its fountain pen writing that reached me a couple of months later. "Come on down when you're ready.

Let us know when you're to arrive." I resigned my job as a radio station reporter immediately.

3

Utter Simplicity

The weather reflected my mood as I returned to Auckland from my first visit to the monastery. The express train from Wellington jolted its way through the Otahuhu junction at dawn, raindrops trickled glumly down the windows of my third-class carriage. Yes, I had discovered my spiritual "Promised Land", but would I ever make it back? Could I finally break free from my hometown's gravitational pull?

The city's streets sounded and felt maniacal; my apartment was cold and dark. I went back to work in the newsroom at full-throttle: chasing fire engines, ambulances and police cars. Well-meaning colleagues placed interesting women in my path.

In the midst of all that I found my way across town to a Catholic bookshop where I bought a silver crucifix and paperback edition of the *Grail Psalter*.[1] I tacked the icon of Love up on the wall in the bedroom that never saw sunshine, just a few feet from a busy, inner-city arterial road. Later in life, a friend remembered my domestic arrangements as "squalid" or "sordid" ... or perhaps both? Nevertheless, this was where irregularly I knelt down and opened my little book of Psalms. I tried haltingly and self-consciously to imitate what I just witnessed morning, noon and night during the week I had spent with my Trappist family-to-be, sequestered many miles south.

"Glory be to the Father, and to the Son, and to the Holy Spirit," I intoned, scarcely able to hear anything above the roar and screech of rush-hour traffic.

Why mention this at all? Because somehow I had managed in a few discombobulated days to pluck out of this completely unfamiliar world the essence

---

[1]. A 1963 translation of the Psalms made from the Hebrew especially for daily sung prayer.

of the contemplative life. Night-and-day adoration of the Son of God, couched in unbelievably ancient Songs of Praise. They were not my own thoughts or words but belonged to Another. And yet, once out in the air, I did "own" them, even more than the dog-eared notebooks full of my strained and overheated poetry.

"My days vanish like smoke; my bones burn like glowing embers; I forget to eat my food … I lift up my eyes to you, to you whose throne is in heaven. As the eyes of slaves look to the hand of their master."[2]

History is replete with the names of women and men who have just walked out of their own lives for God's sake. They've wandered off into wildernesses devoid of pathway and signpost, been ambushed by bandits and demons, haunted by phantom voluptuaries. They "went about in sheepskins and goatskins, destitute, persecuted and mistreated … They wandered in deserts and mountains, and in caves and holes in the ground".[3]

Some disappeared without trace and their stories will only ever be heard in Heaven. But many

---

2. Psalms 102.3-4 123.1-2
3. Hebrews 11.37-38

The Abbot's Shoes

somehow survived, were joined by others and became the founders of houses of prayer that have borne fruit for a thousand years. How could that be? In spite of many dangers and the precariousness of their lives, the routine, relentless chanting of the Psalms (often so mundane in worldly eyes) was the unbreakable "golden string" that led them in "at Heaven's gate".[4]

My time waiting to return was alternately stormy and becalmed. Sometimes I seemed to be rushing at my desired destination; at others I was completely motionless and going nowhere. I cannot remember how diligent I was about praying the Hours then. But I do recall how desperate I was to just get back on the overnight train and, via the Manawatu Gorge, return to the monastery.

How did I ever make it? Only by God clinging to me, and my clinging to that "golden string". Its utter simplicity and poverty of spirit can evoke disbelief and even disdain from spiritual connoisseurs. But for all who ever dare to "live to pray", what appears to be inadequate and even disappointing

---

4. "Jerusalem" William Blake. "The Oxford Book of Mystical Verse" (Nicholson & Lee, eds, 1917)

will always keep us safe and draw us home ... at last.

4

Father Louis

I had not long been at the monastery when one of the seniors stopped me and said, "We're not really all that interested in Thomas Merton here!" It felt like a rather gratuitous slap in the face. Yes, I was surprised and of course disappointed. But somehow or other it just seemed a bit unnecessary and rather sad.

On the one hand I didn't consider myself a "Merton-ite". But on the other, a particular passage in his classic, spiritual autobiography had touched some indefinable part of my being, and transformed a good idea into a destination … Kopua Road.

The Abbot's Shoes

Towards the end of 1968, I had been out of high school for the best part of a year. I'd already managed to "drop out" of teachers' training college, tried to join a pacifist bee-keeping community, and then taken a job as a post office clerk to pay back my studentship. During one of my meal breaks, I wandered up the city's main street and into a major bookshop. I have no recollection of how it happened, or the thought processes involved, but a short time later I walked out in possession of *The Seven Storey Mountain*.

I read the book immediately, intensely and greedily, and was completely absorbed by the account of the life of the American son of a New Zealand artist. Orphaned in France, Thomas Merton was an intellectual who flirted sincerely with bohemianism and radicalism before coming to faith in Jesus Christ. He then dramatically immolated himself (and his dreams and aspirations) in the "graveyard" of Our Lady of Gethsemani Abbey in Kentucky, USA. There he wrote his life's story under obedience to his abbot, Dom Frederic Dunne. It became a bestseller, thus resurrecting and miraculously fulfilling the youthful, literary aspirations he had "knifed" to join the white-cowled monks and become Father Louis.[1]

The remarkably brief passage that set my monastic pilgrimage rolling is on page 416. It describes the completely prosaic: Gethsemani's novices "milling around in the clatter of washbasins ... eyes full of soap and water"! Only a few words; no compelling ideas. And yet, flint and stone struck, creating a spark. An interest became a plan. Ablaze with enthusiasm, I charged over the road from my workplace and up a flight of stairs to the dingy "drop-in" centre run by a Franciscan friar with whom I had been whiling away some lunchtimes. He chopped me down in full flight with a startlingly violent denunciation of Merton for being some kind of heretic and propagator of error. I crept back to work, but not before getting this angry son of Francis of Assisi to dig out the address for the nearest Trappist abbey ... Our Lady of the Southern Star, a mere few hundred miles away.

At that time in my life, the height and depth of any theology I might have had was, "Lord, save me!"[2] The ins and outs of false accusations of syn-

---

[1]. "The Seven Storey Mountain" recounts that he ripped up and burnt four manuscripts for novels immediately before entering Gethsemani.
[2]. Matthew 14.30

cretism were way over the top of my young head. All I knew was that I had just met someone who seemed to have more than half an idea about how to handle the ideas and ambitions that made my peers look blank and my elders frown. And I wasn't about to relinquish such a one for even the supposed comfort of a fiercely proposed orthodoxy. In fact, as I sat back down at my clerk's desk I thought, "I will go to America and find this Trappist monk and talk to him."

It was not to be. A few days after finishing the book, I read Father Louis' obituary in TIME magazine. The 20/12/68 edition announced his death in an article headlined, "The Death of Two Extraordinary Christians". (The renowned Protestant theologian Karl Barth — mentioned by Merton in his own prolific diaries — had died on the same day.) The news story described my new-found and so quickly lost spiritual director as having "worked hermitlike on his writings in the hills of central Kentucky", where he had generated "a message of love that was ardently Christian". It reported that while he had given "his life to contemplation", he had "found in the Word a command to do".

It took me three more long years to finally reach

Kopua Road. I flailed and floundered around wildly during those "waiting" days, lashed mercilessly by the storms and whirlpools of the "flesh, world and devil". I stayed afloat (only just) by continuing to read some of Merton's 70 books, by crouching at the back of empty churches, and occasionally driving out to the edge of the city to gaze hopefully south, in the general direction of the Hawke's Bay.

Forty years later, as I began to learn all over again how to "live to pray", I dreamt vividly of finally meeting Father Louis in his hermitage in the woods of Gethsemani Abbey. The sun was sinking low and slanting in through a window. I took the top off a bottle of ink on his desk and discovered it contained his blood. As he entered, I hastily put the top back on crookedly, and set it down. He asked what I had been doing. Somewhat apprehensively I told the truth, knowing that any evasion was out of the question. He smiled and we embraced. I could feel underneath his black and white habit some kind of brace for an injured back.

5

Bare Bones

Monastic communities have been likened to Jonah the prophet's whale, in which the contemplative finds himself travelling in "the belly of a paradox" of death and resurrection.[1] This being the case, then the "whale's" skeleton is the Liturgy of the Hours, the Divine Office, which is the regular, communal singing of the Psalms, interspersed with prayers, hymns and Scripture readings.

Living in Our Lady of the Southern Star's guest house I very quickly picked up that these times were the family's heartbeat and pulse. Everything else (farm work or study) was finally incidental,

---

1. "The Sign of Jonas" Thomas Merton (Hollis & Carter, London 1953)

The Abbot's Shoes

important but subsidiary. The day began for the community at 2.30am with the night Office or Vigils. I was enthusiastic to be at long last living (albeit on the periphery) in a monastery. So, getting up in the middle of the night was a novelty and seemed initially quite easy. Having worked as a nightshift reporter the previous year possibly helped me to adjust and adapt.

The church was humble and not at all the great cathedral-like structure many might have expected. The atmosphere was unexpectedly cosy and intimate. A few lights made the bare wooden floor glow golden, and the air always smelt faintly and pleasantly of polish, beeswax and incense. It was not romantic, but real. A small group of weather-beaten, manual labour-hardened men, dropping down again and again upon calloused knees to be about their God-ordained business. They sang on through the nights, in the darkness of faith, praying for all who did not, could not, would not "kneel before the Lord who made" them.[2]

This time I was not alone in the guest house. In fact it was quite busy. Some were regular retreatants; others, school-leavers prospecting the

---

2. Psalm 95.6

possibility of a vocation. No matter the goal, all were confronted by something immense — the contemplative continuum. This unbridgeable and unfathomable River that has flowed forever from Heaven, catching and sweeping both orthodox and eccentric men and women out of their depth and into lives of prayer. It carved a course through Israel's Temple and on out into the wilderness communities of Syria and Egypt's Christian Desert Fathers and Mothers.

In the 6th century, Benedict of Nursia created a Rule to try to bring some form and order to those who risked the River's cataracts and whirlpools. Then 400 years later, Bernard of Clairvaux blasted its then sluggish arteries, renewing its purity and momentum.

To be honest, at this time the best I could do was sense that something yet unseen and unknown was close by, and I needed to find some way of inching closer and closer to "it". This I managed to do microscopically and incrementally, by throwing myself into the Hours and farm work. Through the graciousness of the community, I no longer lurked at the back of the church, but stood in the choir in the last and least place. The monks sang the Psalms together and to one another by standing in two single files facing each other. Every Hour began and ended by our facing the Altar and the icon of the Crucified One. He was the inspiration and consummation of our fire-like fervour, which produced so much heat, yet so little flame and smoke.

But the longer I stayed the more I sensed a very great difference and distance between the atmosphere and routine in the guest house, and what was going on "over the wall". And this discrepancy disquieted me. Finally, one day while working out on the farm with Father Basil, I presumed to tell him about my spiritual discombobulation. I feared an abrupt ending to my pilgrimage. "Is there not some place," I asked, "other than the guest house, where I might live?" Once again this good and holy monk took his time, focusing on some distant object. "Well," he finally said, "I don't really see any great problem with that. I'll see what's to be done."

We returned to grubbing weeds before washing the day's sweat off in a waterhole built by the monks where the Manawatu River collides with a bluff before rushing away through a right-angle turn.

Bare Bones

Father Basil (left) and Father Joseph. Source: *The New Zealand Herald/newspix.co.nz*

6

Fading Away

Some 40 years later, one of the monastery's monks remarked that my shed at the back of the orchard had hardly been "fit for a dog". I was surprised because at the time I certainly hadn't felt like a dog; in fact I was as happy as "a pig in muck". Summer had passed its zenith by the time the eirenic Father Basil came back to me with the offer I accepted immediately. I could live in a room in one of the rough-hewn buildings raised up by the six pioneers he had led to New Zealand from Mt. Melleray Abbey in Ireland in 1954.

I continued to take my meals in the guest house, sing the Psalms in the church, and worked hard on the farm. But I felt happy, having managed to inch a little closer to Kopua's heart ... which nevertheless was still hidden from my view. It seemed to me then that what I longed to see would only become visible as Jack's "chaos and decay" faded out. No doubt it may seem trivial and puerile to many, but the target of my first feeble attempts at asceticism was my hippie hairdo. Many precious months of growth was the 60s symbol of a brave, new world that was to be inaugurated by some sort of revolution. "Make love not war"? The revolution soon lay in clumps at my feet as the abbey's barber set about me with clippers in the community's bathroom. I couldn't have given two hoots about my appearance, nor the wind whistling around my newly exposed ears. In a real way the shaving of my head was sacramental; an "outward and visible sign of inward and spiritual grace".[1]

My contemplative journey had scarcely even begun, but I returned to my shed contented. Something had been started that would not be stopped ... forever. My world now measured about 8 by 12 feet. The workbench by the only window (stained and oily from boot and shoe repairing) was my

---

1. "The Concise Oxford Dictionary"

desk. An old box my seat. A sagging wire-wove my bed. An outside tap, tin washbasin, a small cube of green soap, my bathroom. What was new was the carefully written horarium (the names and times of the Hours) pinned up by my door. They were now the scope and meaning of my life. A gift of guidance from the Guest Master who I sensed probably had serious reservations about the wisdom of letting loose some heretic kid in a remote corner of the enclosure of a Cistercian abbey. Upon reflection, I imagine the whole monastery was a bit nervous about such an intruder. A completely reasonable response, I now think. But it did not show, not so much as a squeak of disapproval or anxiety. Rather, at every turn I met with warmth, kindness and cheerfulness.

One evening in the restful time between the Hours of Vespers and Compline, I was sitting at my desk and noticed a Brother Martin pacing back and forth on a nearby pathway. He kept looking in my direction, so I went out and hailed him. He seemed pleased and ran over to thrust a brown paper bag into my hands. "I thought ye might be hungry ... not getting enough to eat," he burst out in his rich Irish brogue. He took off, not hanging about for any superfluous gratitude. The bag's contents revealed that this authentically saintly man had ransacked the kitchen on the quiet to gather up a tremendous collection of fruit, biscuits and lollies.

Brother Martin was one of the six original pioneers (from Mt. Melleray) who had stood in the fields by Kopua Road and seen not emptiness, but an abbey.[2] Through the next year or so I came to know him a little. He was a monk who "thrashed" himself, working like a navvy on the farm. After he shook your hand, you might feel for the space of some hours you should visit the nearest hospital and check for broken bones. But that was nothing in comparison with the tangible, supernatural strength that emanated from him in the choir during the Offices.

My own father was an exceptionally tough man, who had been tested as an army officer on numerous battlefields during the Second World War (north Africa, Italy, India), and then proved himself as a leader in his city's business community. But he more than met his match in Brother Martin. During his one visit to Kopua, my father attended Sun-

---

2. During those earliest years these men endured physical and emotional hardship as well as social and spiritual vulnerability.

day morning Mass, before returning home with my mother and brother. During the Prayers of Intercession, Brother Martin cut loose with a salvo of heartfelt, rumbling prayers for my family. My father sat in his pew and shed a tear. Later he explained, "That's the only time anyone has ever prayed for me in public."

As they prepared to leave, the pioneer tossed a sack of his finest potatoes into the boot of their car. I heard that my father savoured those spuds. Every mouthful for months was a prayer for a tough guy, from a tough guy.

7

Sea Change

Winter comes with a bustle in the Hawke's Bay. Snow flurries up on the nearby Ruahine Mountains begin to send signals and icy draughts sneak down and out onto the Takapau Plains. "What plans do you have, Brother? It's unlikely you'll last long in your shed through one of our winters." Father Basil's low-key and reasonable question jolted me awake. I'd unconsciously disappeared into my new way of life as if it were permanent. But the community was realistically aware of just how dangerously temporary it really was.

I had no answer. I had no plans. I just wanted to stay, and see what might happen … I guess. My

The Abbot's Shoes

mumbling vagueness and hesitancy were yet again greeted by the uncommon liberality and comprehension of Father Basil, himself exiled here from his beloved Ireland. "You know it may be possible for you to come and live amongst us within the community. I'll have a word with the Abbot. I'll see what's to be done for you."

The days got shorter. The nights became longer and much colder. I woke up one night cold-sweating as screaming possums fought over the desirable warmth in my shed's ceiling. It was not a sound easily recognised by a city-slicker. I thought that a gang of demons had arrived to drag my soul away. What little hair I had left on my head stood on end for the rest of the night.

The guest house seemed not so popular as winter pressed in. Getting up in the middle of the night was no longer a novelty. Farm work was, well, just that ... work. Nevertheless, there was nowhere else I wanted to be or could be. I missed nothing. I pined for no one.

"You do not want to leave too, do you? ... Lord, to whom shall we go?"[1]

As a teenager growing up in the Presbyterian

---

1. John 6.67–68

Church and with a Quaker grandmother, I had a completely unexpected encounter with God that left me "in love" with Jesus of Nazareth. I wanted to live for Him and to serve Him with all of my heart for all of my life. But it mattered little then where I turned or looked for some sense of connection to His People, or avenue of servanthood or ministry. I drew blank after blank and lived carelessly. But then at 18 I read Thomas Merton's autobiography and was completely gripped by an unreasonable determination to find a Trappist monastery and live in it. Out of the question? Utterly impossible? Of course! Absolutely!

On Sunday mornings, after the second Office of the day (Lauds) and before Sunday morning Mass, the whole community usually filed into the chapter room for their weekly business meeting. Sometime after our conversation, Father Basil let me know that the monks were going to consider in such a meeting the possibility of allowing me to join them. The Sunday morning when everything was hanging in the balance for me, I dawdled about the humble cloisters, hovering between the church and my shed. Childishly, I semi-hid as the monks left their meeting, scattering to make their prepara-

The Abbot's Shoes

tions for the week's beginning and completion ... the Eucharist. I was desperate to hear my fate, very afraid I might be on the first train out and back to an oblivion I had only just managed to escape. I had given no thought whatsoever to the practical consequences of my project failing. If I'd ever had a bridge, it had most certainly been burnt.

Preoccupied, I almost walked right through the Abbot. He had an ability to glide around the house, and once or twice I seriously and respectfully suspected him of having the saintly ability to bilocate. "The community has voted on ye, Brother. Ye're to come in here and live with us, do ye know!" Delight was too tame and washed out a word. But my response to the good news stunned my new family. I immediately ran away straight back to Auckland's "dark satanic mills"![2] But not to escape. I needed to tell my own family face to face about the future that even the most devout and pious Catholic parents sometimes could only see as wasteful madness. I returned "home" a week later, and not a day too soon. The monks generally

---

2. From the hymn "And Did Those Feet?" by William Blake (England, 1757–1827)

thought I had bolted, that I would never be seen again.

8

Altogether Different

For the most part Kopua Road runs straight and true from the main road to the railway line; both linking Napier and Palmerston North. I happily walked its miles and then, near the monastery gate, saw Brother Martin and others working nearby in the potato fields. I thought I would detour a little closer to see what was what. I was disarmed and pleased to be greeted effusively. It's hard to imagine the "Prodigal Son" being received more warmly and wholeheartedly than I was that morning.

Back in the guest house I was rather stiffly told that I would have to wait for the Novice Master into whose care I now passed. It was altogether a curious day ... not at all unpleasant, but strange. My status had changed. I had gone from being a bit of a novelty and become a novice. No longer a guest, I was plainly told by the youthful, bright-eyed Novice Master, "From now on, you'll have to do as you're told."

In no time at all, and after a brief "tour" past the scriptorium, refectory and ablution block, my new Master showed me into my "cell". Two things I observed immediately. Someone had clearly worked hard sandpapering and varnishing a "new" table and chair for me. And the view out through my room's louvre windows was stupendous. Snow sparkled on the tops of the Ruahine Ranges; icy silver and gold. I dumped my backpack, and standing alone and still for a long time mused out loud, "I'm here and I'm happy. I just don't care anymore whether I live or die!"

Passing from the "outside" to the "inside" overturned great parts of my life ... beneficially. Intellectually it's a "no-brainer" and easy to say that the perspective of a spectator is altogether and radically different from the participant. But it's another matter entirely to experience such a drastic transition. My life in the shed had been pretty much the same as it now was in the novitiate ... the Hours, meditation in church, hard, manual labour on the farm. Everything was absolutely as I had hoped, and yet? One cold and dull afternoon as I walked along the draughty passageway from our sleeping quarters to the refectory, I realised that I felt very nauseous. Was it something I had eaten? A virus perhaps? I went on feeling sick for quite a while, but told no one. Upon reflection I now believe I was suffering from anxiety. Not that I was aware of worrying about anything in particular. However, at almost every turn so many of my basic life and spiritual assumptions were being gently questioned, patiently dismantled, even overthrown. It is but the basic ABC of the spiritual life. Before we can be authentically attached to God, we must become detached from everything that is not. The brilliant 20th century philosopher and Carmelite martyr Edith Stein explained this when she wrote that if we want to share in the life of Jesus, we must "pass through the death on the Cross like Him".[1]

As a young man I had developed my own "brand" of quite free-wheeling Christianity. It was a shock to be asked by my Novice Master one

---

1. "The Science of the Cross" (ICS Publications, Washington DC 2002)

day how long I was spending praying. Before I had time to formulate a smart answer that probably involved the word "maths", I was peremptorily (but not unkindly) instructed to "go every day to your place in choir, kneel down, and pray for such-and-such a time". I had never realised just how slowly the clock by the bell rope ticked away the minutes. It was indeed humiliating, but salutary, to see myself writ large in the mirror of those often-dreary moments. I very much hope no guests ever watched me kneeling at the front of the church alone. If they did, I trust they were not ever tempted to think that they were observing a holy monk caught up in some mystical moment of rapturous prayer. If only they could have watched from the front and not the back of the church. They probably would have laughed out loud at a kid, grimly watching the clock, praying fervently, not for a noble or tragic "intention", but for the time to be up. Perhaps it was necessary that before I could begin to begin to learn how to pray, I had to discover and feel that there was not one single, prayerful bone anywhere in my six foot four inch body?

9

False Start

It is not true that a Trappist monk digs his own grave, a sod at a time, a day at a time … whilst contemplating his own death with a doleful expression. However you could certainly have heard one say, "Ours is a hard bed to lie on, but a sweet bed to die on!"

As a teenager I had been startled and awakened by the story of Francis of Assisi and his lifelong "love affair" with his Lady Poverty. My quest for something beyond the social and spiritual status quo of the 1960s was much more than adolescent rebellion. It was a serious and deeply felt need to connect with God, by disconnecting from everything that was not. My then critical and shallow view of religion was that it simply and conveniently sanctified the way things had always been, rather than inspiring a crusade for Utopia. I just could not accept that my elders were really serious when they contended and defended that the way things were was "as good as it gets".

At 22 I had no coherent philosophy or theology. But I did have the serious and earnest belief that Jesus of Nazareth and the monastery were the finest Guide and roadmap a man could possibly find, in Heaven and earth. So, I really hit the ground running and took to the monastic life and its traditional asceticism with youthful ferocity. Upon reflection, although they were much too polite to say, I am sure that some of the seniors found my behaviour comedic. I decided that my basic and modest room was much too posh and luxurious a place to launch an all-out, quick-fire assault on Heaven's gates. Surreptitiously I got rid of my mattress, sheets and pillows and replaced them with one sheet of hard board and a blanket. Early mornings were extremely painful; a rugged concoction of stiffness, pain and being frozen. But laced into this was the crazy notion that I was surely progressing swiftly along the "highway of holiness". It would have been nigh on impossible to knock me off this course. During the day I haunted the scriptorium, feeding the flames of my zeal by devouring stories of asceticism and mortification that sounded almost fantastical. Saints who never ate or survived on the Bread of the Altar. Hermits who prayed all night, not noticing the snow falling and piling up on their backs. Contemplatives standing in waist-deep rivers to keep awake for marathons of prayer. These were the inhabitants of my day and night dreams; my inspiration and my mentors.

But every runaway cart deserves a brick wall. Mine was a dose of the flu ... an incredibly sore throat, bronchitis and asthma. Overnight the man of "faith and power" was a child of "paste and flour". The Infirmarian took charge. Mattress, pillow, sheets and blankets were returned. No questions permitted. Stay put! Three square meals a day delivered on a tray. Total humiliation. Plans and schemes of overnight sanctity went up in a cloud of antibiotics, cough mixture and painkillers. I hope that the community had a good, long chuckle. I deserved it.

Later that winter I did have a taste of authentic

asceticism. I had obtained another self-inflicted injury by insisting on wearing light sandals right through the year's coldest months. Very Franciscan, I hoped. Large cracks appeared around my heels, and sure enough one erupted into an ugly and painful infection. *There he goes again. Shortcut saint shoots himself in the foot ... literally.* One afternoon I was due to work on the sheep farm and concluded I just couldn't do it. My Novice Master was (as usual) sympathetic. "I'll talk to 'the Boss'," he said, with a reassuring, "right as rain" tone. I settled down in the small patch of sun left on my bed, ready for another tasty dose of bilocations, incorrupt bodies and stigmatics. Marvellous!

"The Abbot says you're to go out to work. Period!"

I limped heavily off down to Kopua Road and out towards the back of the farm to link up with Father Basil for work. Most of the way I bristled and growled with a mixture of self-pity and indignation. Not unlike self-made men, self-made saints do not take contradiction kindly. As I walked beside the infant Manawatu River I felt something burst in my boot. The terrific pain vanished and the relief was immense. I sat down for a while, washed

False Start

my foot and the pus from my sock, and then continued on for a decent couple of hours chopping ragwort out of the paddocks.

I still have no idea why Father Joseph endured tacks sticking up through the soles of his black shoes. Likewise, I do not understand why he sent me out into the fields to work when I could hardly walk. Do I impute ill will or bad intentions to him? Not in the least. What was he thinking? I'll never know. What I do know is the events of that afternoon did me no harm, but good. Bona fide asceticism is learning to disappear, so that Someone else can appear. John the Baptist understood and lived this foundational truth. Jesus "must become greater; I must become less," John told the crowds, perhaps eager for a glimpse of this locust and honey eating, desert celebrity?[1] Thomas Merton's final public words were, "I will disappear."[2] A few hours later he died, suddenly.

My stagey acts of mortification unhealthily enlarged me. The Abbot's decision creatively diminished me. The goal of the contemplative life

---

1. John 3.30
2. "The Hermitage Journals" John Howard Griffin (Andrews and McMeel, Kansas City 1981

is to "live to pray". This will happen only when we choose to really "become nothing".[3]

---

3. "The Science of the Cross"

False Start

Thomas Merton. *Photograph by John Lyons. Used with permission of the Merton Legacy Trust and the Thomas Merton Center at Bellarmine University, Kentucky.*

10

Hidden Power

A Trappist monk who chooses to hide the fact that he is ill and in pain may well have developed a neurotic love of suffering. However, it is much more likely that he sanely and sincerely believes he is sharing in Christ's Passion.

Viewed from the outside, the sacrificial strand of the contemplative life appears contrarious, even nonsensical. Why a meatless diet? Why the disappearance of certain meals during Lent? Why an abbot's total power to command? Why the ban on speaking from sunset 'til dawn? Why the suffering in silence?

A Christian monk's self-denial should not be

confused with the ascetical practices of other religions. His goal is not enlightenment through the demolition of ego and self, but concern for others, their welfare and salvation. It has everything to do with the belief and custom of the early Church that prayer and self-denial go hand in hand.[1] Thomas Merton's first abbot, Frederic Dunne, taught his community that "prayer with sacrifice is infallibly answered".[2]

The Irishness of the monastery on Kopua Road meant that this vital part of its life was not shouted from the roof-tops. Their easygoing modesty and self-deprecating humour made sure of that. One autumn morning as I walked through the orchard, I was greeted by the Guest Master, Father Declan, who seemed full of the joys of spring.

"The truck is down by the river," he said. "Would you like to have a look?" Well, why not, I thought, failing to register anything special about the truck being down by the river. To cut a long story short, while he was opening a gate, the large ex-army lorry he had been driving had taken off

---

1. Acts 13.3 14.23 Mark 9.29 Some manuscripts read: "This kind can come out only by prayer and fasting."
2. "The Less Travelled Road" Rev. M. Raymond (The Bruce Publishing Company, Milwaukee 1953)

by itself. It had shot past the startled priest, hurtled down a steep hill, cut a spectacular swathe through head-high blackberry bushes and finally come to a steaming, shuddering halt with half its engine submerged in the river. No shouting or yelling. No banner headlines. Leave the drama to others. And so it was in all of our life together, especially when it came to being forgetful of oneself for the sake of others.

Many today may scoff at the story of 7th century Celtic soldier-turned-monk Cuthbert of Lindisfarne being helped by wild otters during his frequent all-night prayer vigils. To "fast" one's comfort and sleep by standing in freezing sea water to keep awake doesn't put too much strain on my imagination. Cuthbert's determination to pray for others more effectively for longer periods and his modus operandi are comfortably biblical and contemplative as far as I am concerned. And as for the otters warming his frozen feet with their breath and drying them with their fur? Well, why not? I certainly observed in the monastery that as the veil between Heaven and earth grew diaphanous, all creatures (domestic and wild) seemed more at ease about us.

The Abbot's Shoes

What may appear to be showy acts in obedience to our Lord's demand that anyone who would follow Him "must deny himself and take up his cross daily"[3] were, in fact, something other … hidden, profound, powerful. The Trappists of Takapau didn't flash it about. But it was going on all the time like an underground stream of pellucid purity and beauty. And you could only learn it by osmosis. Perhaps by just watching the way a monk rested for a moment on his fencing shovel, then later the same day held aloft the Cup of Salvation. His bearing and air communicated everything; more than a complete library of mystical theology ever could.

Edith Stein simply called it "helping Christ carry his cross". It's a way of life that in no way questions or denies "that the work of salvation has been accomplished". Writing in the shadow of Nazi Germany's death camps which ultimately claimed her life too, she said, "Only children of grace can in fact be bearers of Christ's cross. Only in union with the divine Head does human suffering take on expiatory power."[4]

---

3. Luke 9.23
4. www.essays.quotidiana.org/stein/ "Love of the Cross" (ICS Publications, Washington DC)

The monastery is such a long way away from Jerusalem and Calvary; separated by thousands of miles and years. And yet because the Crucified cleaves to the poor men of that place, and they to him, the meaning of their sufferings is transformed. Their constant, silent hymn of praise is "the sufferings of Christ flow over into our lives ... indeed we share in his sufferings ... for the sake of his body which is the church".[5]

---

5. 2 Corinthians 1.5 Romans 8.17 Colossians 1.24

11

Not Alone

The year before I went to live in the monastery, I had worked and dwelt in the inner city. My flat was wedged in a semi-industrial part of town, with shops and pubs also close by. There was a dance hall directly across the street, and most nights of the week bands blared and thumped away the hours. The worst spin-off was the multiple uses revellers made of the dingy alleyway right outside my bedroom window. I frequently woke to the sound of people urinating against the outside wall of my sleeping quarters. On busy nights I was often disturbed by other noises that could have been associated with homicide or copulation. I never knew, and I tried hard not to care too much.

I hasten to add that my own life at this time was far from angelic. But the urban environment and atmosphere heightened my great sense of isolation and longing to "escape" to Kopua Road. At the time I was a "blind" man, failing to see even the most obvious tokens of God's encouragement … sometimes dropped literally at my feet. The side road nearest my home was St. Benedict's Street, and I often cut down it on my way to various escapades around the town that usually involved the over-consumption of liquor.

Sitting in the novitiate classroom I was to learn that the 6th century Italian Benedict of Nursia was considered the founder and father of Western monasticism. If only I had known that back then, especially on those days when I blankly traipsed down "his" street searching for happiness which invariably intensified my feelings of inner vacuity and even desolation. This strong sense of alienation and disconnection from God's People was powerfully addressed and began to be resolved in 1972 in a way I never anticipated. A Novice Master — Father Benedict.

The longer I lived within the enclosure, slowly but surely the solid group of cowl-clothed monks began to separate into particular individuals … faces, voices, personalities, talents and foibles. Father Benedict came into focus for me with a rush and a roar. The community had placed me in his care. So he was responsible for me; in charge of me. A startling new idea for a 60s kid, used to a culture of independent Protestantism, and the "do your own thing" hippie revolution. In many respects the relationship between a novice master and a novice is one of master and disciple. I certainly didn't feel any pressure to "leave my brain at the door" of the novitiate. Nevertheless, I learnt quite quickly that if it came to a battle of wills, it was going to be Benedict's way or "the highway".

As I understand it now, there are very crudely speaking two kinds of novice master: the gatekeeper and the catalyst. The gatekeeper is on the lookout for reasons why his disciple is not suitable. The catalyst searches for ways and means to weave his (even awkward, unsuitable) novice into the fabric of his contemplative community. Father Benedict was an outstanding catalyst. He was not physically imposing, but he punched well above his weight. He was perhaps a little informal, but he did not ever suffer fools gladly. You always knew exactly where you stood. But if you showed him one ounce or modest flicker of spiritual hunger or vision, then nothing was too difficult for him. Heaven and earth were there to be moved, if necessary out of the way, in his quest to help you discover that unmarked path some call a vocation.

Morning by morning, after milking the cows and hosing down the yard, I barged into Father Benedict's study, oblivious to whatever he might be doing. There I would launch into some fiery, ill-considered rant about whatever might be occupying my mind. I knew very well at times that I was annoying him immensely. But my need to talk things out was strong and I felt that for the first time I was heard. My (usually selfish) raves were neither meaningless nor futile. Slowly but surely under this regime I began to crawl and inch forward in the only direction that made any sense at all, both then and now … to "live to pray".

I remember one particularly painful occasion when I had worked myself into a complete lather and agony of scrupulosity. I knelt down at the door of my master's study; going around in ever-diminishing circles, trying to communicate what I feared was about to catapult me out of the monastery or into Hell. Finally he interrupted and declared (a little impatiently), "I don't really know what you're talking about, but God knows and He forgives you." There is a particular grace, which I believe God grants parents for their children, and masters for their disciples. It clothes the unspoken and unspeakable with words and gives the incomprehensible shape and texture. Spiritual progress is either impossible or imaginary without this grace and without such fathers or mothers who have the wit and courage to entrust themselves (and their charges) to the uncharted currents and "blindness" of faith.

We later walked to the side chapel where the master celebrated the Eucharist, and the disciple served. He had poured oil into my heart; I now poured water onto his hands. Together we dissolved into the mystery of "This is My Body ... This is My Blood!"

12

A Thorny Issue

I became a Roman Catholic at Kopua because I wanted to be one of the monks. I did not want to become a monk because I was a Roman Catholic. It seemed obvious to me, but few others have ever easily shared this point of view. In fact my attitude to being one of God's People has caused more difficulties than it resolves. But I am a Christian, not because of my adherence to the Church, but because of my determination to try to live my life grafted into the Person of Jesus Christ. And I will love all of His People, because they are His and therefore beloved.

For those who "live to pray", the Mass, Eucharist,

Communion, Lord's Supper is the consummation of the Hours. The Psalms sung, prayers prayed, Scriptures read are then and there heaped up, dissolved and ignited by His words, "This is My Body ... My Blood!" As one thing they fly (like an angel of the Lord) up to Heaven "in the flame of the altar".[1] My Scottish Presbyterian forebears thought daily Communion dangerous "Romanism". So they overreacted by instituting their practice of quarterly Communion. In the darkness of those early mornings, I found neither familiarity nor contempt during the monastery's conventual Eucharist. The ring of monks (both priests and brothers), standing within an intimate circle of candlelight, was at once a moment intensely private and yet universal; of earth and Heaven. Deity was disguised as bread and wine; glory veiled by the commonplace; power clothed with utmost vulnerability and fragility.

I know it was no accident that wherever I stood in the circle, I was always flanked by two much older Brothers. Even after the Renewal of the Second Vatican Council (in the 1960s), these men chose to continue wearing the distinctive "poor"

---

1. Judges 13.20

A Thorny Issue

brown habits of a lay brother. They had built monasteries with their bare hands, and yet were more at ease upon their knees than their work-booted feet. From one I always received the predawn "Kiss of Peace", before passing it on to the other. I am ashamed to say it took me a long time to figure out the reason for their constant presence. These two men had grown up in a religious culture, which had a hierarchy of "classes" ... priests and laity. I am sure they accepted joyfully that their vocation was to "live to pray", but as "woodcutters and water carriers for the entire community".[2] I do not for one moment believe that they felt inferior or saw themselves as second-class citizens. But I do believe that they had developed an eye and sympathy for the outsider and the outlander. What could possibly be more alien to a conservative, Irish cradle-Catholic and Trappist monk than a heretic hippie kid who in almost every area of his life did not yet know his right from his left hand ... and didn't even realise it. I am now sure that they had appointed themselves my spiritual guardians; I was their prayer project. I am sadly sure they were very disappointed and even annoyed on the morn-

---

2. Joshua 9.21

ing I threw my few possessions into a backpack and made a run for it. But I do not doubt that their prayers continued unabated, and perhaps even intensified.

How did they react 10 years later when a newspaper article announced I was "not a Catholic"? I don't know. I certainly felt embarrassed and cut off. I can only hope they did not feel that I had just been some sort of spiritual or religious gadfly. I do not believe I have ever knowingly or willingly broken any of the promises I have made to God and His People. I have tried to be as faithful as I know how to be, wherever I have found myself at different times in my Christian life. I refuse to give up loving and belonging to the Presbyterians of my childhood, the Quakers of my adolescence, or the Pentecostals of my adulthood. And moreover I will never deny that I am still "Brother Peter", the most unlikely, unsuitable, unruly Trappist novice imaginable.

The issue of loyalty to a particular party or tribe of the People of God, in spite of current ecumenical "make-nice", remains as thorny as ever. I would have to say that I feel always and everywhere an outsider. As a Catholic, I was a "convert", and a lit-

A Thorny Issue

tle suspect. As a Pentecostal, I was highly suspect, because I "had been" a Catholic. Later, returning to serve the Presbyterians pastorally, I was impressively suspect, being both Catholic and Pentecostal.

It is a thorny issue and certainly not irrelevant. But the significance of denominational and doctrinal allegiance pales into ashen unimportance when compared to personal devotion to the Person of our Lord Jesus Christ. I like to think of my two "older brothers" continuing to pray for me even now "with unveiled faces" reflecting "the Lord's glory ... transformed into his likeness".[3] And I dare to hope that they might now understand when I take as my own the words of Brother Roger, a founder of the Protestant Monastery of Taizé in France. When he was received into fellowship with the Bishop of Rome, he said, "I have found my identity as a Christian by reconciling within myself the faith of my origins with the mystery of the Catholic Faith, without breaking fellowship with anyone."[4]

Today it matters little to me what church I'm

---

3. 2 Corinthians 3.18
4. Roger Schutz (1915–2005). His testimony is generally accepted as "oral". Another form is: "I have found my proper Christian identity in reconciling in myself the faith of my past with the mystery of the Catholic Faith, without rupturing communion with anyone."

in. If we kneel down to sing together the "Our Father", I always disappear, back into that warm, incensed circle of light to stand between Brother Thomas and Brother Martin. And if I'm passing a Catholic church I will go in and sit awhile before the Bread of the Altar. For if God became a Man, is it really so hard to believe that that Man becomes Bread for us all?

13

Real World

Over the years many people have said to me, "Weren't you bored being so isolated away in a monastery? Didn't you feel in danger of shrivelling up intellectually, being so cut off from real life?" My answer is always an unequivocal, "No!" The contrary was true. I met more interesting people during my sojourn at Kopua, than I had ever encountered previously.

Not only does a contemplative community generate its own stimulating spiritual and intellectual life, but also, it is an interesting place that attracts interesting people like a magnet. An important part of Benedictine monastic spirituality is hospitality.

The Abbot's Shoes

Benedict went so far as to say in his Rule, that all guests "shall be welcomed as Christ". He insisted that his monks should be especially careful how they treated poor people and pilgrims, because "in them Christ is all the more received".[1]

Southern Star's guest house was plain, but had all the comforts of home, and there was a cottage where married couples and families could stay too. Everything was supplied, including three substantial meals a day. There was no charge, but it was understood that guests should make some kind of monetary contribution, as they were able.

One aspect of the community's reception of guests, that impressed me was their openness to having particular visitors come into the enclosure and address them, either in the scriptorium or the chapter room. Sometimes this generosity could backfire. I recall being confronted on one occasion by a somewhat intoxicated gentleman with a dodgy accent. My journalist's antennae were working overtime as this fellow slurred his way through a rambling, slightly comprehensible talk about Orthodox monasticism. My family listened politely and attentively, and even complimented

---

1. www.osb.org/rb/

him with some questions, which he did not seem to grasp. Afterwards I suggested to Father Benedict that the speaker was a fake and from "another planet". "Oh!" he replied. "Do you think so?" His response was more of a rebuke than a question! But these other-worldly men were not naïve! They were just kind and tolerant, in ways that the world appears to have forgotten. Anyway it didn't really seem to matter, as no great harm had been done. And it had livened up an evening.

On another occasion a Pentecostal pastor was admitted and "heard" ... a friend of a friend of the community. As a (then) "former" Protestant, I found this visitor's spiel embarrassing and humiliating. I say "spiel" because this undoubtedly earnest man's speech was impersonal and formulaic. I had the feeling that we were listening to something others had heard on many previous occasions. He seemed to have no appreciation that he was privileged to be within our sanctuary, or that he was surrounded by a finely-tuned, intelligent, mature and powerful prayer "engine", disguised as a group of farmers. He assumed we all needed to be "saved", and so began by preaching at us to that end. He then moved on to proclaim the novel wonders of being "baptised in the Holy Spirit"[2], as if spirituality was a new or strange concept for contemplatives. Our speaker's "coup de grace" (finishing stroke) was a heavy-handed condemnation of our being "worshippers of Mary". I later heard the Prior respectfully and restrainedly attempting to explain to him the difference between worship and love. He wasn't listening.

Other visitors to Kopua were more memorable and for happier reasons. The local Anglican bishop came by one afternoon with his wife to say "Farewell" before moving on to a more senior role in his Church. The Trappists and he were clearly friends. He had made his episcopal ordination retreat with them some years earlier. Out of respect for his married state the whole community left their enclosure and packed into the guest house, complete with bishop and wife. "Mrs. Bishop" looked a little taken aback. I suspect now that their visit might have been intended to be more along the lines of, "Let's pop in and say goodbye to the Abbot". To find yourself suddenly confined in quite a small space, cheek by jowl with a whole community of 25 Trappists must have felt a bit dif-

---

2. John 1.33

ferent, and perhaps even daunting? But the atmosphere was charged with warmth and affection. It was clear to me that the community really loved this man, and the feeling seemed to be mutual. I can remember nothing of what was said that afternoon, but I can still feel that shared respect, admiration and devotion.

How is it that in some circumstances Christians from differing denominations find it so easy to love one another? And yet in others, squabbling (and sometimes palpable contempt) appears effortless? If a Christian is someone who is inching slowly but surely closer and closer to Jesus, like a frozen man seeking warmth from a fire, then we will see the others similarly gathered in a very particular way. Those close to us in this circle of faith will only be visible to us in His light. Believers on the opposite side of this fire will also only be illuminated by His flames, and that view will also be through the shimmering heat. Some would argue that this brings distortion. I would want to say that this is what it means for us to "walk in the light".[3] Could it be that we fail to recognise others as being "the body of the Lord"[4] because we have become severed from

---

3. 1 John 1.7

our Head? And do we risk this detachment whenever we venture to camp around anyone or anything other than the Nazarene Himself? It is hard to imagine a more fearful kind of "judgement"[5] than being so disjoined and yet remain insensible.

---

4. 1 Corinthians 11.29
5. Ibid.

14

At Play

There is nothing especially romantic about smashing the ice covering the tops of water troughs, whilst walking through the chilly darkness to milk cows. It is not in the least bit poetical digging fence-post holes through root-ridden dirt, drenched from head to foot and in the teeth of a driving hail-gale. And yet, manual labour in a contemplative community is an essential and mysterious component. It is something more than fulfilling Benedict of Nursia's dictum that they "are truly monks when they live by the labour of their hands as did our fathers and the Apostles".[1] Thomas Mer-

---

1. www.osb.org/rb/

ton intuited this unfathomable when he wrote that however hard a Trappist monk's manual toil might be, it could be experienced as play. He understood right at the dawning of his own vocation that treating work as play made an abbey "a kind of earthly paradise".[2]

How else to explain a gentle joyfulness, suffusing the whole Kopua community as it turns out to pick potatoes on a winter's afternoon, in the chilly shadows of a windbreak of massive macrocarpa trees. There was still ice mixed into the freshly turned soil. The crude belts to hold our harvesting sacks soon began to pull and cut, even into the youngest and sturdiest backs. But suddenly a half-rotten and stinking potato ripped past my right ear at high speed. A little indignantly I straightened up and turned to identify my assailant … an immensely pleased, broadly-grinning "Boss"! In an instant some kind of silent permission was granted and the air filled with flying vegetable missiles … some aimed with remarkable precision, and travelling painfully fast. The bombardment died down as quickly as it had flared up. We bent back to our

---

2. "The Intimate Merton" Ed. Patrick Hart & Jonathan Montaldo (Harper-Collins, NY 2000)

toil, but the field full of doubled-up labourers was clothed in an atmosphere of kindly playfulness. Needless to say further fights erupted, but the Abbot seemed to grow weary and wary as the afternoon wore on, whilst others surprisingly warmed to their sport.

It was not that we treated our farm work frivolously or carelessly. But I would say that when the whole community turned out, including the "retired", there was a sense that each monk's contribution was valuable, but not essential. If there was a can to be carried, then we bore it all together. Thus the burden of this or that task was distributed and seemed to become almost lightweight. Perhaps this was what led to the possibility of our becoming light-hearted … even as we grubbed for potatoes in a frozen field.

During the following summer, we all turned out together again. This time to gather, load and stack heavy bales of hay, ready for winter-feed. Again, a sense of occasion and celebration took over; a fair bit of levity got mixed into the tough job of lifting and "flicking" the bales up onto the back of our truck. I paused to rest for a moment and caught sight of a guest, standing stock still beside the gate into our paddock. He was indeed a "prince" of the Church; a representative of the Pope no less. I do not believe it was my imagination, but this solitary figure emanated a palpable sense of wistfulness and longing. I believe he would have given almost anything to rip off his clerical collar and run out to join God's Trappist "kids", living to pray, and playing at work.

One summer evening, we straggled home from different parts of the farm after an intensely hot and dry day of hard work on the land. Some of us seemed to arrive simultaneously in the dusty yard that was hidden behind the guest house inside the enclosure. A soccer ball appeared out of nowhere. I'd certainly never seen it around before, and for just a few minutes, clouds of dust flew up, monks toed the ball like professional players and yells of delight and reproach filled the air. And yet but a short time later, we were gathered in the church to slip silently and easily back beneath the surface of the River of God. Seamlessly gliding from work which was play, to pray as our work.

"O God, come to our assistance. O Lord, make haste to help us."

15

An Apprentice

A novice is really a "child" who belongs to the whole monastic family. And within the community there will be particular "masters" to whom he is apprenticed ... formally or informally. The primary and most obvious is the novice master. And whether he is (in his own mind) a gatekeeper or a catalyst, will sometimes literally make or break those in his care.

During my brief monastic "career", I had two novice masters. The first, Father Benedict, was an enthusiastic and devout catalyst. But he suddenly disappeared out into the guest house. Perhaps, as a New Zealander, he was considered more apt and

The Abbot's Shoes

capable of relating to the quite steady stream of "homegrown" enquirers and aspirers. I ignorantly and unkindly suspected that my (by now) spiritual director had been given the "heave-ho" for representing some kind of threat to the Establishment. His replacement did little to assuage my doubts. This senior was a cultured, prayerful and humorous man, but right from the start he made it pretty clear that I really was the wrong fellow in the wrong place. And how did I handle that? Exactly like any "know-all" 22 year old. I launched myself into ways of relating and behaving that guaranteed his prognosis was confirmed on an almost daily basis. The point is that (sadly) I now have little sense of this godly and scholarly monk having made much of an impact on my life. Whereas others who had no immediate or official role to play in my formation, shaped me significantly and creatively.

Every Tuesday afternoon I went out to work, fencing with the Abbot. I do not know whether it was by design or accident, but in spite of his health concerns we always worked in the most difficult places. Sometimes in the winter-cold shadow of trees, chopping our way slowly and painfully through one root obstruction after another. At

An Apprentice

other times we toiled in some boggy piece of paddock, where freshly-dug holes filled up with muddy water, and posts were impossible to anchor. I wasn't used to older Christian leaders applying and occupying themselves in such crude labour voluntarily. I was impressed, and have continued to be so. There was something timeless and poignant about that scene; the highest and the lowest, the greatest and the least, talking animatedly and endlessly, backs bent to a job few would have considered plum. Father Joseph was, I now realise, an extraordinarily humble man. He tolerated my endless and idealistic yapping, interrupting now and again, to drop out a one-line pearl. These gems usually arrived as a question, signed off with his characteristic verbal flourish, "Do ye know?"

I knew that the monastery's carpenter, Brother Thomas, was "retired". I also knew that he had built more than one monastery, and our beautiful church furniture. And I had been advised to give him plenty of space, perhaps like a pup giving a veteran working dog a wide berth. Most afternoons, I could see him sitting in his workshop, which was just across a corridor from my own room. I ventured into the "lion's den". I and others need not have worried. I spent hours mucking around there, yarning. Eventually with considerable help from this "master", I managed to carve a crude Madonna on a hunk of wood we hacked off an old fence post. As I write I am able to look at it, and I think of the beautiful Mother and her most beautiful Child, our Saviour. And I also think of "Tommy" and the mysterious process of spiritual osmosis that always occurred during our afternoons together. Any momentary irritation he may have felt at being invaded by a former heretic, he managed to disguise with amazing skill. His profound devotion and modesty humbled me, and still do.

Sadly, this story has an ending of which I am ashamed. Later in the year, Brother Thomas made me a small stool; a work of art. It enabled me to kneel for longer before the little silver crucifix that hung on the wall of my room. On the day I "ran away", I just abandoned it … as I did the whole community. No doubt whoever inherited my room would have returned it to the workshop. How I now wish I had had at least the common decency to do this myself and also say, "Goodbye and thank you … master."

There is so much of value and importance given

An Apprentice

to us in classrooms and lecture halls. But there are other things we can learn ... profound, mysterious, imperative. We can only receive these by absorption, like moisture through our skin. And this usually happens as we slipstream a spiritual "master", as we humble ourselves for a time and choose to live in and become their shadows.

16

Life Together

If the singing of the Hours is a contemplative community's skeleton, then the common life, as well as manual labour, is the flesh that clothes the frame. Bernard of Clairvaux viewed a communal life for his disciples as being the most normal and healthiest source of their necessary asceticism or mortification. Hourly, petty irritations or commonplace frictions always occur when human beings live together 24/7 in close confines. And when it comes to slowly but surely learning to say "no" to oneself and "yes" to Jesus Christ and others, this regime outstrips all others ... fasting, hair shirts, rock-hard beds included.

For me, this aspect (although vital) is not what is of ultimate importance. In a monastery, our Lord Jesus Christ is the hearth and the fire, and the monks gather around Him as His family. Their way of life is neither accidental nor merely convenient; it is prophetical. This "life together" is an undying, incarnational witness that there is for us a familial lifestyle prescribed by God. It is hostile to that disintegrating one, grimly pedaled by corporate and media moguls. It is also to be the pattern for life to which we will return before history's ultimate crisis and The Day.

"When I think of the wisdom and scope of his plan I fall down on my knees and pray to the Father of all the great family of God — some of them already in heaven and some down here on earth."[1]

We usually took our modest breakfast of bread, jam, cheese, hot milk any time between 3.30–4.30 in the morning. So by 9 o'clock after milking cows, hosing out the yard and walking back to the enclosure, I was very hungry. However, our family life (not written or recognised by the timetable) made provision for me to hide in the warm kitchen and take a bonus breakfast of toast and a hot drink.

---

1. Ephesians 3.14–15 (Living Bible)

Life Together

From time to time, other monks dropped by, creating an ambience remarkable for its joyful conviviality, as well as lively, enlightening conversation. This kitchen "club" became so popular and well-attended that it had to be quietly closed down ... by "the Boss". Nevertheless, my (catalyst) Novice Master discreetly counselled me to "pull my head in" for a while, then pick up where I left off ... alone. Later, one-by-one, the "club" reformed. The cooks never complained.

During the two or so years before I shifted to Kopua Road, I had worked as a journalist and lived alone. So I had a good idea of what unhealthy solitude and loneliness felt like. And I had also learnt the danger and pitfalls of phony belonging to this or that crowd or clique. Every member of a monastic community has duties and responsibilities. Mine were milking cows, general farm labouring, and spending Mondays doing all of the laundry for the monks and the guest house. I enjoyed my jobs and their immediate practicality. But most especially I enjoyed having duties because that meant I had a place in the family. I belonged.

And just as one's duties could be totally mundane or lacking so-called importance, so the sense and joy of community came home at humdrum, even trivial times. Cultivating togetherness was not necessary. It was not unusual to be served a main meal by one of the house's theologians; scholars cleaned the toilets; a senior might painstakingly translate portions of a new book from German into English for a novice; an occasional overseas news magazine mysteriously materialised in an ex-journalist's room.

Perhaps my most heartwarming and human memory of "life together" began with Father Benedict asking if I smoked. I told him I could take it or leave it. "Well," he said, "if you need a cigarette, go and see the Procurator." I did, and was promptly supplied with all the makings ... tobacco, papers and matches. "Oh," said the reverend keeper of the stores, "when you do smoke, go out behind the long shed at the back of the enclosure."

One afternoon after work, I beetled eagerly along the orchard path, past my old shed door and ducked behind the building. I barreled straight into the small Trappist smoking group. What could I do but hide my surprise at its existence and its diverse, interesting membership, roll one and light up. But that's not the punchline of this particular tale. I also joined the dots and realised that for the duration of my occupancy of the shed, the smoking group had obviously relocated, out of respect for my privacy. They quietly accepted this disruption to be kind to some Protestant kid's vague need for solitude, as his search for God intensified. These were serious-minded and devoted men, who had made immense sacrifices for many years, in order to "live to pray". And yet, so far as I could see, they held all of their rights and privileges lightly. They were spiritually supple; able to bend and flex to accommodate and make space for each other ... even the least in their midst.

"Whatever you did for one of the least of these brothers of mine, you did for me."[2]

---

[2]. Matthew 25.40

17

Just Thinking

From time to time my mother used to say, "Sometimes Peter sits and thinks. Sometimes he just sits!" In the monastery, in the pre-dawn darkness the whole community would gather every day for an hour of meditation. I do not remember anyone ever saying much to me about this by way of highfalutin philosophy or technique. I'm glad of that. As a result, I sometimes just sat there and thought. At other times I just sat ... and watched the clock, lit by the one light always left on in the church, tick off the minutes.

This time was not totally devoid of diversion or entertainment. One elderly Brother's digestion had been manifestly affected by a lifetime of Trappist fare. I'm not sure if it was the time of day or the great stillness, but his gastric malfunction would often manifest itself in a string of extraordinary, hiccoughing eructations. I childishly waited in the fond hope that others might join him to create a symphony of even more tuneful blasts. I report such events respectfully, as I was always profoundly reassured and encouraged by such routine, easygoing outbreaks of earthiness within our sanctuary.

For some people, meditation is understood as a quest for enlightenment or even a supernatural experience. Particular methods and postures are advocated. Sometimes the goal appears to be trying to empty out the contents of your head or mind in the belief or hope that the void or vacuum will be filled with light or wisdom ... or whatever else is being sought. Such esoteric possibilities flew well over my head. The memory that I prize of these times, some forty years on, is much more down to earth.

For me, it was an event of the greatest beauty, simplicity and impressiveness. The whole monastic family (young and old, brilliant and unexceptional, Heaven or earth-bound) sat together for a while each day, just to think. A radical event really, especially in the context of modern-day culture, which for the most part is completely blind to our own mindlessness. During the 20th century, intelligent civilisation was attacked simultaneously by two equally vile kinds of totalitarianism. Today, thoughtful culture is under a more subtle siege from the tyranny of the majority's opinion and the lust for acclaim (at any price?) in the wild, weird world of social media.

Our one hour of meditation was not preceded by directions or instructions. It was not followed by small-group brainstorming sessions, either. We just sat or knelt, still and silent, to think by ourselves and for ourselves, together. However, it would be a great mistake to think that this practice and routine occurred disconnected from anything else. Well did the Psalmist exclaim, "Oh, how I love your law! I meditate on it all day long."[1] Apart from the earliest Hour, the Eucharist with its Scripture readings, and meditation, the remainder of our early morning time was taken up by "Lectio Divina" or holy reading. The Bible was the most important book we read. The community aspired to be wor-

---

1. Psalm 119.97&99

thy sons of their founder, Bernard, for whom the Scriptures were "verbum salutis" — the word of salvation! When the Mellifluous Doctor[2] preached, his sermons were awash with the sacred Text or its echoes.

Before I emigrated to the Hawke's Bay, I visited the Presbyterian minister who was a friend of my family. I told him of my plans, but was surprised when he became grave and urged me to be sure to take away with me a copy of the Reformer John Calvin's "Institutes of the Christian Religion". I declined his well-intentioned counsel. Even though I had been raised on the usual Protestant horror stories about Catholicism, I expected security, and not danger, at my desired destination. This was confirmed during my time living in the shed at the back of the enclosure. One afternoon I was wandering in the orchard when Father Kieran, the Prior and one of the community's scholars, approached me. "Do you have a Bible to read?" he asked. I shuffled and muttered that I did not. I had thought up until then that the Psalms we sang our way through every day and other readings from the Bible were sufficient. "Well," he said kindly, "I was

---

2. His speech was said to have been as "smooth, sweet and healthy" as honey.

only asking because I'd heard that you Protestants weren't reading the Bible much anymore!" This was not some religious cheap shot. It was a genuine gesture of pastoral concern, and I was not in the least put out. In fact it struck me as funny, and was one of my earliest experiences of the irony and paradox that abound in the no-man's land between Catholicism and Protestantism, which I now inhabit.

I was later to learn that John Calvin had in fact been a great admirer of Bernard, favourably citing him many times in his own writing, and affirming this contemplative as one of the "ancient Doctors of the Church". I would like to think that Calvin the Frenchman might have been impressed by the sons of Bernard the Frenchman, sitting together in the dark, savouring and ruminating on "the bread of angels"[3] until the "juice" and goodness had been thoroughly extracted and absorbed. Perhaps a little dyspeptic musicality was somehow appropriate after all.

---

3. Psalm 78.25

18

The Hermit

One afternoon I was kneeling in the church. A door opened and closed behind me, as somebody I did not see came in. What struck me was that the sense of "presence" was significantly more and other than just someone else. At the time, I was still slowly navigating my way from the outermost edge of the monastery and so did not know who this was, save that he was a monk. I had already glimpsed him on odd occasions as I made my way to work at the back of the farm, on the other side of the river that ran right through our property. He would often be standing beside our pathway, and

The Abbot's Shoes

usually exchanged a few quiet words with Father Basil.

As time went by, more and more faces came into focus for me, and names were attached. This mystery monk who had aroused my curiosity was Father Maurus, "the Hermit".

A cenobite is a contemplative who lives in a community. A hermit is a contemplative who lives alone. Although strictly speaking Trappists are cenobites, there is provision for seniors to live as hermits within their monastery's precincts. Early in his contemplative career, Thomas Merton became famous for his spiritual autobiography. However, later in his life he became equally well known for his struggle to be permitted to live as a hermit. He succeeded, and observed later that he had not gone away into greater solitude to seek God. He believed that a hermitage would be the place where God could find him.

Father Maurus lived near the river in a primitive little cottage. It was well hidden, down behind a very steep bank. This place was treeless and austere. I am surprised he did not freeze to death during the winter. Occasionally I saw the Abbot loping across the fields, obviously heading to the hermitage to care for his "son". Now and again, the Hermit quietly slipped back into our midst for a few days, for reasons a novice was deservedly not privy to. I think that somehow or other I intuited his importance. Not as some kind of poetical, romantic figure, but a constant, blunt reminder of why Southern Star Abbey existed at all. Father Maurus was living out on the farthest reach of the contemplative vocation. He lived to pray at the "end of the road", along which the rest of us were supposed to be advancing. As in every way of life, it is possible in our spiritual journey too, to find a comfortable plateau with a view, and camp there. Of course we are full of the very best intentions to get up and get going again ... just as soon as we've had a rest. The tiny fibrolite hermitage sat like Isaiah the Prophet's "flagstaff on a mountaintop".[1] It was a terrible reproach to those who might be hiding from their own vocation; a profound encouragement to all who felt utterly devoid of strength and yet continued to be haunted by the enigmatic "allure into the desert".[2]

Through the kindness of Father Benedict, I did

---

1. Isaiah 30.17
2. Hosea 2.14

once follow the Abbot's path; down Kopua Road, past the red cabin where the monastery's pioneers camped in extraordinarily close quarters, over a couple of fences and down the steep incline to the hermitage. My afternoon with the Hermit was a confrontation with divine paradox. Unhealthy illusions were gently broken; spiritual bedrock uncovered. As the chilly autumn wind off the Ruahines began to snarl around our shelter, Father Maurus seemed to both diminish and become substantial, the more we talked. I was nervous and disconcerted to hear a senior speak so unabashedly and eloquently about his own sense of insignificance, self-doubt and even desolation. His rough, cracking voice and the poverty of his accommodation added poignancy to the scene, which I can only describe as beautiful. I was surprised that he listened so intently and actually seemed to be interested in my half-baked answers to his animated enquiries. I realised that he might have seemed to others a broken man; like a sailing ship driven onto rocks and pounded by a ferocious storm. What I saw was someone like an old fireplace with blackened bricks and buckling iron grate. But in this hearth's heart was a fire that was skin-blisteringly hot.

The Hermit

As I said goodbye, I asked for his blessing and knelt down upon the muddy piece of sacking on the hut's doorstep. His voice and hands were rough and heavy. But the grace of God flowed ... fluid, tangible, eternal. When I had climbed back up the bank to head for home, I stopped and turned for one last look. The Hermit had disappeared. The wind blew. The river flowed. All were swallowed up in the falling darkness.

"The desert and the parched land will be glad ... The burning sand will become a pool, and the thirsty ground bubbling springs ... And a highway will be there; it will be called the Way of Holiness."[3]

---

3. Isaiah 35.1, 7–8

19

For Everyone

After the novelty of getting up so early to sing Vigils had worn off and temperatures fell to freezing, I just sat hunched in my choir stall wanting to throw up. It was a kind of timeless zone; neither late at night nor early in the morning. Nurses call it the "dying time". I had known night-shift reporters lie down on the floor of the newsroom at that hour, overwhelmed by a leaden need to sleep.

In spite of this Hour's pain, it allowed me my first glimpse (as if out of the corner of my eye) of the reality that enclosed contemplatives do not abandon their fellow men. "It is in the name of all that we stand before the living God." Our hearts, a Trappist abbot once taught, had to be "large enough to embrace the whole world ... you and I have the entire world in our care". But not just as some abstract concept or vague, pious hope. Our cause was meant to be nothing less than "union with Christ". Out of this alone, the contemplative "gives to all of the fullness of the grace which he knows and by which he is possessed ... He shares the breath of the Spirit, the Comforter, and becomes himself a comforter (and) lights and warms the world".[1]

Our house of prayer seemed very small, swallowed up and swaddled by the night. Few visitors came into our public church at such an hour. We were utterly alone. A tiny vessel adrift on an ocean. A flickering pin-head of light, so very far away from everyone and everything, "dead" and buried in the darkness. And yet, it was then and there that I most keenly felt and believed that even our sometimes distracted, threadbare praying, actually "worked". Our tired voices and ancient, oft-repeated repentings and yearnings were given

---

1. "The Carthusian Order Statutes" (Book 4, Chapter 31) www.chartreux.org, "The Less Travelled Road" Rev. M. Raymond (The Bruce Publishing Company, Milwaukee 1953), "A Carthusian Speaks" www.transfiguration.chartreux.org

wings to fly and fill the mouths of others. Most were unknown to us. Many were probably infinitely more needy and desperate than we could ever dream of being.

The consummate Reformed theologian Karl Barth spoke of our prayers reaching God through the mouth of Jesus "inasmuch as he enables us to draw near and be heard".[2] I have not doubted that as I stood and knelt among Bernard's Son-burnt brethren, my mouth and theirs brimmed with so much more than our own private supplications and thanksgivings. It's a remarkably subversive proposition that the unseen, uncelebrated, unproductive contemplative utters petitions that can traverse the whole world, igniting inextinguishable fires of valid and meaningful prayer, even for those who dare not pray or completely eschew it.

It is a brilliant, beautiful but supernatural idea. Perhaps that is why contemplative communities effortlessly provoke ridicule and offence, even from their "friends". In the 1960s, an English prelate caused a furore when he fulminated against "perfectly healthy monks who are priests and who never go out to work in a parish".[3]

---

2. "Prayer and Preaching" Karl Barth (SCM Press, London 1964)

The Abbot's Shoes

For as long as the monastery was my home, some of the monks remained a complete mystery to me. They had withdrawn further into our already secluded family. It would be too easy to see them as strange. They might only occasionally sing an Hour, and they attended to their duties and chores in isolation. In the "normal" world, they might be rushed off to visit the doctor. If life did become unbearable or impossible for such a one, I certainly witnessed the brotherhood's warm, practical humanity and determination to care for them.

And yet I wonder now if perhaps some of these men, whom others might well have dismissed as misfits on the run from reality, were actually fulfilling their contemplative vocations. Had their lives become so totally suffused with God over so many years that every aspect of their daily routine was no longer merely prayerful, but prayer itself?

Perhaps the small, elderly brother mutely splitting firewood and stacking it in a buckling, corrugated-iron water tank was heard in Heaven more compellingly than the rest of us put together. Maybe there comes a time when the one who lives

---

3. "The Hidden Ground of Love" Thomas Merton (Farrar Straus Giroux, New York 1958)

to pray at last steps over an invisible threshold and into a place where liturgical form, word and gesture dissolve. Where feeding scraps of stale bread to a young magpie translates into intercession that is as fervent as it is unobserved, as effective as it is inexplicable.

The Scriptures understand that sometimes people become prayer, and their silent eloquence reminds us that "the world which we can see has come into being through principles which are invisible".[4]

---

4. Psalm 109.4 (KJV) Hebrews 11.3 (JB Phillips NT)

20

Joy Unspeakable

As winter stretched itself icily out over us, aspects of my life became gruelling, even a bit grim. I was finding it almost impossible to keep warm. In the early morning darkness, when I walked down to open up the milking shed, it felt so cold I thought I could vomit. My hands usually bled while I was working in the fields. I felt ashamed when I lost concentration and drifted off into a daydream or nothingness, whilst singing the Hours in the church. If I did manage to wake up at 2.15 in the morning, remaining conscious became more and more of a struggle. But still, there was nowhere else I wanted to be; nothing else I wanted to do.

The Abbot's Shoes

Of course, it was meant to be a rigorously self-denying life. Hadn't Bernard of Clairvaux warned those who aspired to the contemplative life that if "you desire to live in this house, leave your body behind; only spirits can enter here"? But a monastery is not meant to be a spiritual boot camp to pulverise our humanity and produce remarkable feats of ascetical gymnastics. Nor is it to be some sort of hothouse to cultivate all kinds of rare and wondrous mystical experiences and spiritual effects. The great contemplative masters have always taught their disciples to eschew the like. Spain's incomparable 16th century mystic John of the Cross urged teachers to "wean" their disciples from "all visions and locutions" and impress upon them "the necessity of dwelling in the darkness of faith".[1] And more recently, the Carmelite martyr Edith Stein wrote that the "essential" to which we are called is "union with God", which is not necessarily accompanied by anything "extraordinary".[2]

I believe absolutely, that so far as God is concerned the contemplative life is for the most part "ordinary". But it may be punctuated by sudden

---

1. "The Ascent of Mount Carmel" (Christian Classics Ethereal Library)
2. "Self Portrait in Letters 1916–1942" Edith Stein (ICS Publications, Washington DC 1993)

blasts of divine sweetness so unpredictable and undeserved as to appear inappropriate, even embarrassing. One Sunday afternoon I had walked alone far out into the woods at the back of the monastery. Whilst stumbling through an especially dank copse, I was suddenly "stung" by a very strong sense of malevolence and horror from which I literally ran. As I headed for the safety of home, unbidden and completely out of the blue, a great surge and tide of joyous confidence that all would be well flushed and suffused my soul. I think, oblivious to all else, I actually skipped along the path, smiling and babbling gratitude out loud. Then, out of the corner of my eye I saw that I was being observed by one of the seniors. He remained completely still and said nothing. I ducked my head and scuttled off, fearing that my frivolity would be disapproved of. Many years later that monk told me he had never forgotten the scene, and had enjoyed (even envied) my happiness.

What are we to make of these unbidden, unexpected, undeserved "gracelets"? Do we need to make anything of them at all? Do we ever understand how to fly by pulling the wings off butterflies? Do parched fields make a study of the sweet

The Abbot's Shoes

summer rain? Do microscopic creatures analyse the sun's kindly warmth in the wintertime?

So far as I was able to make out then, there was at least something especially important about the close, hourly juxtaposition of prayer and manual labour. Woven together, and esteemed equally, they did seem to create a kind of chemistry. The more immediate their proximity, the thinner the veil between Heaven and earth perhaps? Presumably there had been some particular and special reason for Benedict of Nursia instructing his followers to view and prize prayer and work as one and the same; to accept that their prayer was work, and that their toil in a monastery's fields was prayer.

One Sunday afternoon in the church we were worshipping upon our knees with a hymn of adoration: "Fair are the meadows, fairer still the woodland, robed in the blooming garb of spring; Jesus is fairer, Jesus is purer, Who makes the woeful heart to sing." As we bowed down together and sang of His beauty, I found myself thinking about how pure His mother Mary must have been to be so "highly favoured" as to be chosen to be "the mother of my Lord".[3] There then came crashing in upon

---

3. Luke 1.28&43

me a great, swelling sorrow for all of the wrong that I was; all of the harm I had ever done to others. It was like a violent squall. Sudden and escalating, forcing hot tears out of my eyes, to splash down before me onto the bare wooden floor. This storm of grief also contained joy; something overdue and very important was happening.

The community accepted this visible, emotional outburst by politely ignoring it. The sinking sun set fire to the church's interior. We filed off to the refectory for our supper, where the Prior chased and crushed a fleeing mouse with his substantial Irish foot. An individual monk might well from time to time be upended and shaken to the core by a spiritual earthquake. But his security lies in the ordinariness of his life and his brethren. They will quietly, politely humble him or lift him up and carry him for a while, without complaint or impatience.

A monastery is like a bird's nest. It is fabricated and woven together out of material that is commonplace, provisional, overlooked. But what appears at first glance to be just some rickety contraption of mud and spit is in fact a choice vessel that is as beautiful as it is fragile as it is alive. "We have this treasure in jars of clay."[4]

---

4. 2 Corinthians 4.7

21

Pear Seeds

Was it the absence of a radio or television? I do not know. But from time to time my senses were inundated and almost completely overwhelmed by the unremarkable and commonplace. Were such moments spiritual or mystical? Who could tell? Certainly not me. And yet, I was nevertheless on the receiving end of such epiphanies.

Almost half a century later, I clearly remember those times of heightened sensitivity taking place during None. It was the briefest Office and, being almost immediately after our early afternoon nap, challenging to get to on time. After midday dinner, we took to our beds for the traditional siesta. A blanket of immense stillness and silence descended upon Our Lady of the Southern Star for more than an hour. I found that if I did fall asleep, it was torture waking up and dragging my drugged self to a cup of tea and then back into church.

"O God, come to my assistance. O Lord, make haste to help us" was so much more than this Hour's introit. "Jesus, please help me not to just lie down on the floor right here and fall back into the warm oblivion of sleep."

But paradoxically this Hour of "affliction" often ended in something akin to bliss. Finally, turning back to the Altar we sang, "How great is your name, O Lord, in all the earth. For you have made for yourself a worthy dwelling place, in the Virgin Mary." Then in the briefest of pauses before our dismissal with the Abbot's blessing, earth collided with Heaven, or did Heaven simply invade us? I do not know. For those few seconds everything remained normal, but became extraordinary. The church's window frames and glass, the metal paths, fields, fences and twisted-pine windbreaks outside, were suffused to shimmer with transcendence. Nothing had actually changed. But for a few moments everything was rendered so completely different as to seem to be other.

This is the world where trees and rivers "clap their hands", mountains sing, and the road metal beneath our boots cries out, "Blessed is the king who comes in the name of the Lord".[1]

Eastern Europe's 17th century Jewish holy men (Hasidim) knew well this other and yet completely our world. For them the sacred imbued every created thing that surrounded them. There was divinity and holiness in the way a tree shrugged off a withered leaf to flutter and spin to the ground.

In our Lord "all things hold together" and He is "sustaining all things by his powerful word".[2] Perhaps then we should constantly lean forward and into our little lives, always expecting that at any moment He will "flame out, like shining from shook foil".[3]

The afternoon walk to work on the sheep farm could still be just a weary trudge. Awkward gates opened and closed in the same old difficult way, and the red shearing shed continued to be filled

---

1. Isaiah 55.12 Psalm 98.8 Luke 19.38-40
2. Colossians 1.17 Hebrews 1.3
3. "Gerard Manley Hopkins. Poems and Prose" (Penguin Books, England 1985)

The Abbot's Shoes

with a rich fragrance of dung and lanolin. But that was not all. Everything remained as it was, or seemed to be ... ordinary, commonplace, mundane. And yet?

When the Holy Spirit came upon Mary and the power of the Most High overshadowed her, God was conceived in her virginal womb.[4] And? And the divine was then restored in a flash to its rightful place ... in the core and at the heart of all created things. Dull and sullen evil forever deposed to the periphery of everything, there to wheeze out its vile and nihilistic threats.

"The seed of God is in us ... the seed of a pear tree grows into a pear tree ... the seed of God into God."[5]

---

4. Luke 1.35 Matthew 1.20
5. "Meister Eckhart. The Essential Sermons, Commentaries, Treatises, and Defense" (Paulist Press, New Jersey 1981)

22

Pathways

The final Hour of our Trappist day was Compline. It was not drawn out, but I always found it a profound and restful Office, concluding with the memorable hymn, "Shield us Lord in our waking hours. Watch over us while we are asleep, that we may watch with Christ and rest peacefully."

But for many of the Kopua monks it was not the end of the day. My first post-Compline venture into the church was a revelation. In the almost pitch darkness I kept stumbling upon individuals sequestered to pray in places usually left vacant during the day. I realised that it was important for these nocturnal contemplatives to be able to pray differently in different places at different times. In other words, whilst accepting the obvious and necessary regimentation of a timetable and schedule of Psalms, they also wholeheartedly embraced the responsibility of their personal spiritual freedom. I especially remember covertly watching the Abbot and Father Basil at such times. Strange to say it was a guilty pleasure watching these two seniors. I couldn't help staring because they seemed to me to be dissolving before my eyes; they, the Wood of the Altar and its Bread, becoming indistinguishably one and Other. This I had no way of understanding, but coveted. I always hastily averted my eyes, because I felt embarrassed, as if I was spying on them, observing something intimate, private, too holy to be looked at.

One evening, on the other side of the church, a hidden Father John burst out, suddenly and briefly, in "tongues"; a language neither he nor I understood.[1] I had been told that he was involved in what was then called the Charismatic Renewal Movement, so I was not completely sideswiped by this manifestation. A few years later I too came to pro-

---

1. Glossalalia is the "gift of tongues" spoken of in Scripture. E.g. Acts 2.4 and 1 Corinthians 12.10.

foundly value this experience and "gift of prayer". But on that night it seemed to me to be somehow or other over the top! It certainly took a while for my hair to stop standing up. Nevertheless, I treasured this spiritual ambush, because once again I was confronted by Kopua's humility and open-heartedness. Here were men, backed up by almost a thousand years of Cistercian spirituality, nevertheless willing to engage a renewal movement then untested by history, which carried bits and pieces of cultural baggage (social and political conservatism?) I could not easily connect to Scripture.

In recent years, throughout the whole of the Body of Christ, there has been an upsurge of interest in "spirituality"; the different pathways of prayer and spiritual experience along which Jesus may lead individuals back to God.

The sun-seared Desert Fathers and Mothers majored on asceticism and mortification in their spirituality, whilst apostolic Benedict emphasised community life and scholarship. Prophetic Bernard called his Cistercians to be above all else ardent and extravagant lovers of Christ, their Bridegroom. Soaring Teresa of Avila summoned her followers to storm the "Interior Castle" of their souls, barefooted and at "night". Diminutive Thérèse of Lisieux found her "little way" and "short-cut to heaven" by resolving to be "smaller than ever".[2]

Today many of the different, great contemplative movements treat the spirituality of their particular founders with extreme reverence, much as a carpenter following his architect's drawings down to the finest detail. There are "charisms", history and culture that must be preserved, renewed and freshly walked out by every succeeding generation. Nevertheless, the monks of Kopua set in my faith foundations a vital appreciation of that spiritual liberty we automatically inherit as sons and daughters of God. So, for some, one spirituality will be the sum and total of their life of prayer. But for others, such will be navigation lights (sometimes, but not always close by) to prevent our shipwreck and motivate us to keep on crawling towards The Light.

For a week in autumn, we made a retreat as a community, which was conducted by a priest from another, more activist and evangelical religious order. I was surprised and grateful to be included in what amounted to a kind of monastic

---

2. "Autobiography of a Saint" (Collins, Glasgow 1958)

holiday, with only essential work and duties being maintained. Our Retreat Master spoke passionately to us of the value and benefits of free or extempore prayer in a group setting. The atmosphere seemed somewhat hesitant, even awkward, when he suggested we take some time to put this into practice. Some duly or dutifully prayed spontaneously, out loud. Others stayed very quiet indeed. I was confused. Amongst many evangelical Protestants such meetings were not just normal, but considered the "only" way to really pray. At that time I much preferred silent, mental prayer. I'd had my fill as a teenager of gatherings where the intercession agenda appeared to be set by whoever was able to pray longest and loudest.

But that aside, along with Father John's glossalalia, the community's slightly nervous venture into free prayer both moved and chastened me. I have never forgotten that sometimes as Christians we have to be humble and courageous enough to follow Jesus along ruts worn deep by the feet of countless saints who have already travelled that particular path. But my Kopua fathers also taught me that we will at times also have to be humble and courageous enough to follow Him where there are no footprints, no track, no roadway; where we might not feel in the least bit comfortable, confident or at ease.

"Your path led through the sea, your way through the mighty waters, though your footprints were not seen."[3]

---

[3]. Psalm 77.19

23

Prophet's Death

On the dull, grey afternoon of Monday, October 23, a tiny typewritten note appeared on the noticeboard outside the refectory. Its smallness drew my attention, but its message was massive … for me. It announced bluntly and bleakly that James K. Baxter, one of New Zealand's most celebrated poets, had died suddenly in Auckland the previous evening. We had not been personal friends, having met only by chance on a couple of occasions. Nevertheless, it is no exaggeration to say that I felt shattered. One of my significant life-navigation lights had been untimely snuffed out. He was 46.

Jim Baxter, or "Hemi" to his closest friends and

followers, had gone in late 1969 to live alone in a cottage beside the Whanganui River in the village of Jerusalem-Hiruharama. It had impressive, even formidable history, having been the place where Mother Suzanne Aubert founded the Sisters of Compassion in 1892. He went there with a view to trying to live with others more co-operatively, embracing physical and intellectual poverty, and to "worship God and work on the land".[1] The poet's literary output over the next three years was prodigious and prolific, and included *Jerusalem Daybook*, *Autumn Testament*, *Jerusalem Sonnets* and *Thoughts About The Holy Spirit*. My destination was always going to be the monastery at Kopua, and not the Jerusalem Commune that had gathered around Jim. Nevertheless, I read him avidly, and was always eager for news of whatever might be going on up the River Road. These Jerusalem poems and essays resonated with me because they were indigenous and because they were essentially contemplative. It was as if Kopua and Baxter were slaking a profound thirst from the same spring; their tone and temperature were identical.

---

1. "The Life of James K. Baxter" Frank McKay (Oxford University Press, Auckland 1990)

Prophet's Death

James K. Baxter, June 1972. *Photo credit: Otago Daily Times*

This should not really come as any sort of a surprise to anyone. Jim began visiting Our Lady of the

The Abbot's Shoes

Southern Star Abbey in the late 1950s, and the community became known as "old friends". To his confidant, the scholarly and urbane Dominican priest, Eugene O'Sullivan, he wrote that he thought of the Cistercians he met at Kopua as "God-loving, Irishmen with faces like children".[2] By the time Kopua was my home, the Jerusalem Commune had for the most part flowered. But a remnant still lived together in the village, and some came across to the monastery from time to time … usually at Jim's prompting. I lived in continuous hope that he might show up one day. By mid-1972 the strongly prophetic aspect of his make-up, writing and lifestyle had become apparent. Opinion was, not unusually, strongly divided. It would not be unfair to say that those who wished to be affronted or cynical could always locate plenty of fuel for their fires. It was abundantly provided by reporters looking for headlines, and also by the religious bush telegraph. I preferred the calmer judgement of his friend and official biographer, the Marist priest Frank McKay, when he wrote that

---

2. "Selected Poems of James K. Baxter" Ed. Paul Millar (Auckland University Press 2010)

Prophet's Death

the poet was a prophet, whose "weakness like his strength was always of the heart".[3]

While still in the depths of winter, I set off for work one afternoon, well-swaddled to oppose the snowy blasts off the mountains. I cut down the side of the guest house and glimpsed from a distance a John the Baptist-like profile, standing and waiting at the front door. I stopped and turned and for a few moments we stared at each other in silence. I made the snap decision to continue on to work, confident that this visitor would be staying, and would almost certainly speak to the whole community that night. I tore into the afternoon's graft with extra vigour, anticipating an historic evening. I loved the monastic life of Kopua very much, but was already agitating for some Clairvaux-like reform. Could there not be some new expression of the ancient contemplative River more able to engage the young pilgrims who had laid siege Jerusalem's poet-seer? Back inside the enclosure that evening I was told that James K. Baxter had indeed visited, but left. No more information was forthcoming. Even the optimistic and radical Father Benedict had little to say on the subject. I

---

3. "Autumn Testament" James K. Baxter (Price Milburn, Wellington 1972)

felt cheated. So, the death notice in October was like an unkind wind blowing an important door closed ... forever. Many years later, when reading Father McKay's finely tuned, supportive biography, I read some significant "news". Sometime in 1971, Jim had publicly considered founding a new commune, just a few miles down the road from the monastery, in Takapau. Reading between the lines it was to be another sincere attempt to implement the "vision", which would take seriously into account lessons learned in Jerusalem. I will never know what was discussed or with whom that afternoon in the guest house parlour. Perhaps just some old friend dropping in to say hello to other old friends. Or maybe old friends failed each other that day, as we all so often do.

24

The Tangi

At first glance it's hard to imagine two more different worlds; a Trappist enclosure, and a remote, rural marae, which has suddenly become the focus of national attention and grief.

Throughout the day after the news of Jim Baxter's death had reached the monastery, I was in a turmoil of indecision. I desperately wanted to try to get out and across to Jerusalem for whatever was going to occur. But the community seemed to me to be strangely quiet about the event that was preoccupying me. While I mowed the enclosure lawns that afternoon, the Prior approached and asked what I wanted to do about "Baxter and

Jerusalem". I launched into a bit of a rave about how I wanted to go, but anticipated not being allowed. "Well," he said, "I think you might be doing us all a bit of a disservice. I'll talk to the Abbot." He returned surprisingly quickly. "You're to go! We'll drop you out on the highway to catch the evening bus into Palmerston North. There's some food for you in the kitchen to take with you."

I felt as if I'd been suddenly fired out of a gun; sitting on the bus eating my supper out of a generously-stocked paper bag. The monastery no longer seemed to exist. That night I hitched a ride with a friend, further west to Whanganui, then on up the winding, rough River Road. My friend, a schoolteacher, had been an early, earnest and devout core member of the commune. He seemed a little reluctant to go to Jim's tangi, perhaps anxious it might be hijacked by other interests. I was profoundly grateful that he set aside his own grief and understandable reservations and made it possible for me to say goodbye.

The body of one who had really burnt himself to a cinder, fighting to create a "cell of good living in a corrupt society"[1], arrived in the middle of the

---

1. "The Life of James K. Baxter"

night. For me, the hours that followed disappeared in a welter of sounds and faces; speeches, songs, weeping. I woke up the next morning, having slept on a hall floor, blanketless, fully clothed. I just lay there stunned and watching; a beautiful, elderly Maori woman was brushing her long hair, as if there was nothing more important to do; as if she had all the time in the world to do it.

Crowds of people continued to arrive; to be called onto the marae, to pay their respects to the dead prophet, "resting" on the ground inside a tent. I was anxious, disorientated; outside Jonah's whale, and feeling it. This was a little offset by famous faces coming into focus for me. I sat at a bench eating some dubious porridge, all the while eavesdropping on conversations; one between a handful of New Zealand's literati … a novelist of considerable stature and others I recognised as poets. I was in a sea of strangers, but the grapevine worked well. Now and again I was asked if I was from the monastery. The enquirers seemed pleased that I was!

That afternoon the Requiem Mass was celebrated out of doors, and the 800 or so mourners climbed the steep track to the grave. The air was

The Abbot's Shoes

poignantly thick and awash with all the sweet aromas of spring; the promise of a new season, even as we were mourning and celebrating the untimely, sudden end of another. By that evening I was back in Palmerston North at the bus depot. "Kopua Road," I told the driver. "Are you one of the monks?" he asked, not unkindly. "Yes," I said. "Well, get on. There'll be no charge for you tonight." I sat in the front seat, dozing, and grateful. I wasn't sure if I had had enough money to pay the fare anyway.

Some time later I squatted down in the dark on the side of Kopua Road. I had a few miles to walk, but just wanted some kind of hiatus; a significant pause before I got back home. In the stillness, farm animals chomped and belched nearby, and the stars shone brilliantly overhead. I was very glad that I had been to Jerusalem — to see Jim, to embrace his widow and his daughter and son. They had seemed so frail, as if the slightest puff of wind might carry them away forever. I was pleased to have some Hiruharama dust (literally) in between my toes. Grateful, too, for the crowds who had pilgrim-ed to a prophet's funeral. I optimistically took this as a great sign that there was a remnant in

The Tangi

my country who were grateful, and prepared to be struck and disturbed by prophecy personified.

But I also felt terribly sad as I tiptoed back into my little room. I had gone alone from the community, and had not been accompanied by any of Jim's old friends. I think that their presence would have meant a great deal to the multitudes who had flooded into that tiny riverside settlement for 24 hours. Somehow or other, the knowledge that the distance between our two "worlds" was in fact only paper-thin would have consoled the grieving. The silent monks and the barefoot jongleur, "son" of Francis of Assisi, ate at the same table, sipped the same cup. For as Jim had earlier written to Eugene O'Sullivan (of the Cistercians of Kopua), "They're my brothers, man."[2]

---

2. "Selected Poems of James K. Baxter"

25

Radical Politics

Towards the end of 1972, a General Election was held in New Zealand. Officialdom invaded our sanctuary. A polling booth was set up in the guest house, but I did not vote. Nevertheless, I was pleased with the outcome and the installation of a socialist Government, under the leadership of the former ferry boat stoker, "Big Norm" Kirk. During the previous year, I had interviewed this Prime Minister-in-waiting whilst working as a journalist for a city radio station. He was a giant of a man, self- and well-educated, humble, a gentle revolutionary. But he did not have to win me over. I had already committed myself to his revolution, but employing different methods.

By the time I had left school I was a Christian, and it had always seemed quite normal to me to be as a consequence, a communitarian and pacifist. In the late 60s I regularly marched in anti-war demonstrations, hung around the edges of a Communist youth group, and corresponded with people living in communes in different parts of the country. I was always a bit taken aback when churchgoers I met gasped and tut-tutted over my non-conformity. But for me, my course of action was as plain as the Gospels, especially the "Beatitudes" and the rest of Matthew 5.

Sometime during 1970–71, US military forces in Vietnam decided that the best way to win that war was by saturation-bombing neighbouring countries. The grainy, black and white news footage on TV, coupled with the statistics of death (11 million gallons of Agent Orange laying waste a seventh of Vietnam's total land area.), turned my stomach and my mind over. I recall sitting in my dank apartment late at night and concluding, "All the marching, all the writing, all the campaigning in the world, isn't going to stop this insanity, brutality and carnage!" For a split-second I sat in quietness and somehow intuited that the most powerful, significant and influential action I could take to change the course of this kind of history, was to hide in a monastery. There I could become the tiniest part of God's way of turning the tide, achieving the impossible, "raising the dead"! Some years later, while reading Thomas Merton's diaries[1] I discovered that he had been similarly moved and inspired during his first visit to the Abbey of Our Lady of Gethsemani in Kentucky in 1941. He realised that the monastery that was going to be his home for the next 27 years was "the centre" of the United States. He saw that this house that sheltered an army upon its knees, was "holding the country together ... keeping the universe from cracking in pieces and falling apart"!

I made the leap of faith back then (as I continue to do now), that to disappear out of this world and to "die" slowly in prayer for others upon our faces, puts us (as the Carmelite Edith Stein believed) "at all fronts, wherever there is grief".[2] At Kopua Monastery I could help prevent bombs falling on

---

1. "The Intimate Merton" (Harper Collins, NY 2000)
2. "Ave Crux, Spes Unica" (ICS Publications, Washington DC 1939)

The Abbot's Shoes

Southeast Asia, and at the same time live a purer form of socialism than even Big Norm could inspire and legislate.

In choir we stood, bowed and knelt together in the "death zone" of 3am ... the night all but over, the dawn yet far off. We prayed for everyone and anyone; those who could not or would not cry out to the only One who can hear, comprehend, reply. What could possibly be more meaningful and more substantial than feeling the breathless Wind crossing our Psalm-chapped lips? A raging Wind that has "knocked tyrants off their high horses"; the gentlest Wind that has "pulled victims out of the mud"![3]

Cradle-to-grave "welfare-ism" flourished among the Trappists of Kopua Road. There were no "rich" to resent handouts to the "undeserving" poor. We were all poor, and yet lacked nothing. No matter our age or stage, status or standing, productivity or usefulness, every monk slept in a warm, clean bed, ate three good meals every day, and was cared for when unwell. We were more than adequately clothed (especially out in the fields), and had a glorious array of books to read, sufficient to last many

---

3. Luke 1.52 (The Message Bible)

lifetimes. And the elderly were not slung out on the street, or banished to rest homes. Their place and identity in the family was completely secure. For me, seeing retired Brothers Thomas and Albert out for an afternoon ramble was a vital and vivid reminder that sometimes "just being" is more than enough, so far as God is concerned.

Long before the "armies" of Marx and Lenin marched to foment class warfare, the Crucified's contemplatives were already living the dream. For any young person who had radical aspirations, life in such a society was actually revolutionary. And to kneel in prayer was not a posture or gesture of resignation or passivity. It was ultimate political activism.

26

No Ladders

I intend no disrespect whatsoever to my Protestant upbringing. My Presbyterian forefathers would no doubt bristle at any suggestion of hierarchy within their kirk. Nevertheless, I came to adulthood with the distinct impression that significance and success in the world somehow or other translated into importance and influence in the Church.

Possibly my eyes deceived me. Perhaps the 1950s were another time and place. Our ministers were all "university men", and elders were very often bank managers, headmasters and prosperous businessmen. Was there anything wrong with that? Probably not. However, it did feel to me then that beginning with Galilean peasants and ending up with "pillars" of social, economic and political respectability was quite an awkward stretch.

The satisfying rejigging of my understanding of authority and influence began with my "meeting" Francis of Assisi when I was still a schoolboy. I was captivated by the story of a wild Italian youth whose encounter with Jesus Christ left him upside-down. In fact it was the world that was completely out of step with its Creator, and the wrong way up. Francis saw himself as a clown of God, performing spiritual somersaults to convince his listeners that their conversion would involve a complete and literal revolution … an absolute volte-face. To be wealthy, Francis lived as a beggar. To be successful, he joined society's outcasts and failures. To be influential, he "buried" himself in a remote cave and lived to pray. And here's the point. Today his name is a byword, and yet who knows the names of the rich and famous, the celebrities of his day?

In the very earliest days of my sojourn at Our Lady of the Southern Star Abbey, I was taken on something of a guided tour and formally introduced to any of the monks we met along the way. When we came to the toilet block, the floor was being scrubbed by a quite nondescript, even dishevelled person, dressed in old brown overalls. Clearly not (I thought) a headmaster, bank manager or successful entrepreneur. I was eager to be moving along, keen to meet the house's "important" occupants. In the very best way possible, the toilet cleaner helped to turn my world upside-down. John was a priest and one of the community's scholars. At that time amongst his many responsibilities was the education of those monks destined for the priesthood. Later in his life, he became the abbot.

As I settled in, there arose for me out of my studies a particular question. It had to do with a Latin phrase that was central to the Catholic Worker Movement. It was probably pretty trivial really, but nevertheless important to me at that moment. It was Father John who arrived on my doorstep, assigned to explain and further my monastic education. What struck me was that he didn't just fire an answer off the top of his head. It was clear to me that he had gone to a great deal of trouble to prepare his response. He engaged me carefully, precisely, respectfully. It was as if at that moment my education was the most important thing he had to do. I was impressed, but also disconcerted. My world was slowly being turned over and back up the right way.

In the world, rulers "lord it over" others, and "high officials exercise authority over them". And yet, the Lord of all said that "whoever wants to become great" in the Church, "must be your servant, and whoever wants to be first must be slave of all".[1]

I take this to mean that there is a hierarchy in Heaven that ought to be, hour-by-hour, overthrowing the hierarchies of earth. I caught a glimpse of this phenomenon for the first time in the monastery. In the world (and in the Church too) men and women are arranged in pecking orders; the higher up you climb, the more power and wealth you can possess. But in Heaven there is no such grading. In Heaven, the Lamb stands "in the centre of the throne, encircled" by living creatures, elders and angels.[2] At Kopua Monastery, the Lamb Himself stood in our midst during our daily predawn Eucharist, having "all the marks of a victim slain for sacrifice".[3] We were before Him, but

---

1. Mark 10.42–44
2. Revelation 5.6
3. Revelation 5.6 (The William Barclay New Testament)

not in status-driven, ambition-riven tiers. We huddled in a circle around Him, like soldiers about a fire at night on a midwinter battlefield. Our "offices" and responsibilities differed enormously. But our devotion drove us down onto our faces, where all men and women are truly and finally unique ... and equal.

And so, an abbot-to-be could seamlessly live to pray, clean toilets, pore over his holy books, milk cows, and also painstakingly educate the most unlikely Trappist novice.

The world and the Church (as we commonly now know them) look so much more beautiful upside-down.

27

The Fairer

I had not lived chastely before making my home amongst those who, for the sake of Jesus Christ, were vowed to poverty, chastity, obedience and stability.[1] I was not running away from anyone or anything. Least of all the often-sorrowful archivist, or the perspicacious secretary. I was not especially impressed by a world devoid of women. However, I was relieved, for a while, to be away from myself and the fairer sex. Even as a youth, "blinded" by testosterone, I had learned that I was a selfish and careless sort of fellow in this regard.

---

1. A Cistercian monk commits himself to a particular community in a particular place.

The Abbot's Shoes

At Kopua I found neither paranoia nor weirdness when it came to womankind. For the most part I was amongst men who were noteworthy for being perfectly natural about the opposite sex. Some did leave, marry and have children. On one occasion an academic showed up in the guest house proclaiming the virtues and joys of same-sex relationships. When this was pointed out to the Abbot, I recall that gentleman disappearing off to the Takapau railway station quite promptly. So much for tales of sexual shenanigans and nefariousness in monasteries and convents.

Early one morning in the bathroom I was puzzled by the amount of time one of my brethren and fellow milker of the cows was taking over his personal grooming. For the most part hand basins were for getting rid of dirt; the mirrors served no useful purpose in a monastery, so far as I could see. I have to admit that now and again I did take a look ... to see if I still actually existed. However, my workmate was certainly on a mission with his toilette that cold morning.

This is to be contrasted with the more usual approach to appearance. One afternoon I had my frozen hands in hot water, trying to get the circulation going again. In sped Father Benedict who plunged his head into cold water, parted his dripping hair with an old scrubbing brush, and then took flight. "What was that all about?" I later enquired. "Oh," he said, "my mother has come to visit me."

When I finally got down to the milking shed, the grooming mystery was solved. A little green van was parked outside, and in amongst our cows, intent upon her important job, was the district's herd tester. I surely hope she noticed that there was another in the yard that day ... shaven as clean as a whistle, not a hair out of place, and beaming from ear to ear.

Later in the year it was my turn to face anew the phenomenon and reality of the feminine. On my birthday I was invited out into the guest house by my spiritual director for an impromptu afternoon tea, complete with a cake, and two guests. One, I was told, would be a nun. I had already heard about this woman, as she visited now and again and brought with her books that ordinarily might not have reached us. I knew too that she was very well-educated, cultured and had an influential position in the Church. What others had failed to warn me of was her shattering beauty. I doubt very much if a sledgehammer blow to the side of my head could have been more painful or unnerving. Her refined, elegant and fragrant presence filled the little parlour where we were sitting. I sat and drank my tea and ate my cake (so to speak!), slowly but surely drowning in her loveliness. It is hard to believe she was completely unaware of my state. But what a tragic contrast. I only ever changed my clothes, including my underwear, once a week. My aroma must have been at the very best alarming. My shaven head and stringy, untrimmed beard couldn't have been a good look. And to complete this vision of delight I had read enough to begin a conversation quite impressively, but my conclusions were still half-witted fizzers. I drifted, stunned, back to my cell with its narrow and unyielding bed. And yet, I had no other plans but to remain.

I had only recently received the news that my secretarial ex-girlfriend had ridden her motorbike under a truck and died of her injuries in hospital. She had tried to contact me. Our intermediaries failed to co-operate. I went to serve a special Mass for Father Benedict in which we prayed for this dark-eyed girl. As I knelt on the cold, bare boards, I stared out of the one little window and watched for a few moments the flinty-grey sky. I remembered how we had talked a little over a year earlier, late at night. "The problem with you Christians," she had said, laughingly, "is you talk too much. You need to 'get on the road'!" And so I did.

28

Shadows

A monk of some note once described monasteries as paradises. I doubt very much he was thinking of some kind of human utopia. Perhaps this Trappist had in mind the biblical idea of a beautiful "walled garden" where a king might invite his close friends "in the cool of the day"?[1]

It would be a great mistake to romanticise such houses of prayer and imagine that they are hothouses full of visionaries and ecstatics, living together in blissful peace and harmony. At the same time it would be bizarre to characterise them as

---

1. Genesis 3.8

prisons, occupied by unhappy inadequates. The truth, as ever, is probably somewhere in between.

In the early 1970s the Catholic Church was very much riding the rollercoaster of reform and renewal that had been sparked by the Second Vatican Council, called by Pope John XXIII. Monasteries were neither isolated nor excused from the consequent ongoing process of change and (in some instances) upheaval.

During the winter, a priest came and lived with the community for a few days to facilitate and assist with Kopua's "aggiornamento" (updating). The two novices were quite rightly not included in the "family conferences". We were not vowed to the community, and we also probably didn't know our backsides from our elbows either. I enjoyed the time when all of the monks were shut away together in their chapter room. The abbey seemed spacious and relaxed. I relished roaming around, soaking up the great silence, which nevertheless spoke of days and lives offered up upon the Altar of God. We continued to meet all together to sing the Hours at the usual times. As I walked to the church for Terce-Sext late one morning, I was startled and then abashed to find myself caught in the verbal crossfire of two seniors. A heated conversation had not been concluded by the time the monks came to the end of one of their sessions. Voices were raised, arms waved, cowls flew like flags born aloft by knights riding into battle. I averted my eyes and scurried to my place in choir.

I doubt very much if the argument lasted more than a minute or three. I noted that the combatants had been an Irishman and a New Zealander. Both were younger seniors. Both leaders-to-be. For the rest of the day I felt upset, off balance, as if I'd discovered a family secret I wished I had never learnt. Of course it wasn't the end of the world. In fact it was a good sign; a vital indicator that a movement almost 1000 years old, was alive and kicking, capable of stretching and flexing ... albeit with some protesting creaks and groans.

But it was the end of an illusion, because undoubtedly I had been searching for Eden. But Kopua Monastery was never meant to be Utopia or Shangri La. It was a workplace, inhabited by real men who lived to pray and planned to die at work. They had no fallback position. Powerful medicine for a starry-eyed idealist. But this has always been a controversy and tension in Christianity. Did God

The Abbot's Shoes

become a Man to evacuate us all out and up into Heaven? Or was the Godhead "veiled in flesh" to sanctify humanity, and enable us to enter more fully into our real glory and become "in the image of God" here?[2] Are we in fact called to be angels or human beings?

My brush with monastic realism, in a certain sense opened my eyes to see what had always been there unnoticed ... perhaps blocked out. Monks absent or irregularly in choir. Secret supplies of beer in a hothouse. A cell transformed into an aviary. For some observers, these and other eccentricities would be proof that monasticism is a counter-productive religious ziggurat, deserving Henry VIII-like demolition? Or perhaps it was one of my earliest and most valuable up close and personal encounters with a staple and utterly essential component of biblical faith, that "we have this treasure in jars of clay to show that this all-surpassing power is from God and not from us".[3]

Reality's glancing blow was not very important in itself. Nothing to write home about really. But it did a job and prepared me for a more bruising

---

2. Genesis 1.27
3. 2 Corinthians 4.7

encounter and personal "collision". I was doing some cleaning in the ablution block when my other novitiate comrade came bustling in breathless with excitement. He'd stumbled upon and retreated slowly from a no-holds-barred barney between the Abbot and a senior. This monk (a New Zealander) had been strongly affected by Jim Baxter's concern for those he called "nga mokai" ("fatherless ones"). These were the young people who, for whatever reason, felt that they had no stake in society. Years of monastic discipline and hard labour had not dented or dimmed Brother Francis' idealism. I think he harboured a wild hope that the monastery could, somehow or other, become a refuge or sanctuary for such orphans.

There was really no way, realistically or even idealistically, that this could have happened then. But it was certainly worth a crack. After all, God's prophets cry out endlessly into the howling gale of the status quo, because they must, and not because of the statistics of their success or failure. The ding-dong in the enclosure was really two holy men, each fighting for his own children, each would gladly have died for. God expected nothing less from either of them. The outcome was inevitable.

The Abbot's Shoes

However, the fallout for me was not so creative. As the heated argument was reported to me, at some point the memorable phrase rang out from Father Joseph, "I'll be glad when you and Brother Peter leave this monastery." It had never occurred to me that I would ever leave. I'd waited and dreamed and hoped for three years to call it home. The Abbot's understandable and justified outburst did not unduly offend or disturb me. I wasn't seized by a sudden urge to run.

The force, humanity and realism of the argument did rattle me; it also matured me. All our idols must ultimately topple to the ground and be smashed.

29

Adrift

High summer in the central Hawke's Bay is a season of exaltation. The mountains appear to be dancing far away in the shimmering afternoon heat. The fields seem to doze after being shorn of their harvests, exhaling a breath that is both sweet and warm. The rhythm of the monastery continued without interruption, not unlike the very slow beat of a heavy, old engine idling. The Hours framed our days. The church doors were left open in the evening for the night breezes to enter and produce a perfumed confluence of incense, freshly turned earth, beeswax and cut grass.

The discipline imposed on me to pray endured,

The Abbot's Shoes

and I stayed on my knees ... already rendered knobbly. I cannot report any sense of advancement or improvement in my devotions; neither raptures nor Heavenly visitations. But somehow or other the labour seemed sufficient in itself. What was one to do in the sight of the Suffering Servant, who watched us from the front wall of the church, night-and-day, unsleeping? Perhaps the mere fact that such a recalcitrant knelt there, dumbly waiting, "rewarded in full, his heart's anguish".[1]

I had no thought of wanting to do anything else. My novice master had quietly, and I am sure out of kindness, written to a community of hermits overseas to see if they might receive me. Their reply was not encouraging. "He sounds," they wrote, "spiritually precocious!" Father Benedict remained steadfastly affable and affirming. Nothing, it seemed, was too difficult for him to believe or do for those in his care. I knew too that by this time he was "taking the heat" from some in the community who could see no good reason why I should continue to be in their midst.

I began to drift. But not away from the monastery, or even out to its edges. I discovered a

---

1. Isaiah 53.11 (The Knox Translation)

sanctuary within the sanctuary, as I began to cut some of the Hours to go and sit at the top of a steep bank behind the orchard. An airless and profound stillness and quietness came around me there; it enfolded me and I "disappeared". I always knew when this had happened; the birds and other small creatures considered me with the same concern they might a thistle or a rotting fence post. And after work in the late afternoon I went even further out to the very back of the enclosure where the river was our boundary. Evening after evening I lay semi-submerged in its shallows, washing away the grit of that day's work, daydreaming. Now and again, I was startled awake because the water's "singing" over and through the riverbed sounded like people approaching and chatting animatedly and happily.

I was always pleased and happy to return home. But the cloisters began to seem to me somehow faded, washed out, diminished. At the same time I was aware that Brother Francis was pondering more and more seriously leaving to go and live in Jerusalem. I was also avidly reading the occasional unpolished, mimeographed periodicals put out by some of the new, "experimental" monasteries that were springing up, especially in the United States. In the 1960s, Thomas Merton had begun to articulate what other contemplatives were feeling; a desire to move towards a kind of monasticism that was more supple and less formulaic. Small groups of Trappists and Benedictines had begun to move "out", searching for new "deserts" where they could "find a more authentic and realistic simplicity".[2]

As well, I continued to study and be moved by the story and teachings of the Catholic Worker Movement's founders, Dorothy Day and Peter Maurin.[3] They seemed to me to be on the same page as Thomas Merton and Jim Baxter, emphasising prayer and community, pacifism and social justice. Their object was unashamedly the complete overthrow of society by a revolution ... of the heart. They wanted to fashion the kind of world "where it is easier for people to be good", and wherein "worship, adoration, thanksgiving, suppli-

---

2. "The Hidden Ground of Love" Thomas Merton (Farrar Straus Giroux, NY 1958)
3. Dorothy Day (1897–1980 USA) and Peter Maurin (1877–1949 France & USA) founded the CWM in the 1930s. It was communitarian and fought for social justice according to Christian principles. Dorothy Day said the CWM fed the hungry and sheltered the homeless. But she pointed out that if an observer didn't "pay attention to our prayings", they would "miss the whole point"

cation (to God)", were "the noblest acts of which we are capable".[4]

That was a lot to be going on in one kid's head and heart. A whole lot of powerful spiritual currents, which were not necessarily so easy for Christ's beloved brethren living on Kopua Road to swallow. The anchor of the Hours was holding me … just. But for how much longer?

---

4. http://www.catholicworker.org/dorothyday

30

Runaway

One afternoon I came home from working in the fields, went straight to the guest house and told Father Benedict that I was leaving … now. To be honest I do not really remember very much of our earnest conversation. I do recall, however (because he was not very tall), his feet swinging backwards and forwards as we sat and spoke. They didn't reach the floor. I can also clearly call to mind his plea, "I cannot tell you why, but you must not leave now."

I walked through the church's sacristy and barged into the Abbot's cramped, very humble office. "I'm leaving, Father!" The poor man was startled, jumped up, walked out and disappeared. So, I just sat there (for quite some time) staring out the window, across the vegetable gardens, through the orchard, over the river, and away to the mountains. Father Joseph returned. "Father Basil says to let you go." We then settled down and talked quietly and at length. I can recount no particular words or phrases. But I must say that our conversation was entirely that of a loving parent, counselling and cautioning a child he had always known was bound to run away. I am sure he was torn, feeling also that I ought, somehow or other, to be staying … perhaps just a little bit longer. He also told me that my time in the novitiate would count, and that I could come back and pick up where I had left off. I know he said this out of sheer kindness and soft-heartedness.

That night I posted a very small goodbye letter on the noticeboard outside the refectory. It was as foolish and insensitive as I was young, and the community was right to be offended by it. I patronised them all with some spiritual drivel; an exhortation that they keep on praying, while this adolescent cognoscente ran off to "save" the world.

I slept soundly that night. With the benefit of

Runaway

hindsight (and later conversations) I am sure that others did not. I believe that Father Benedict would have crawled (as was his custom) under a bench in choir to pray ... for me to change my mind and stay. And the Abbot no doubt thudded down onto his knees before climbing into his bed (as was his nightly habit) to reproach himself for having failed me. I have never, ever believed that he did.

Early next morning I served Father Benedict as he celebrated the Eucharist in a tiny chapel just off the sacristy inside the enclosure. He had often asked me to do this, knowing how fervently I longed to frequent the Altar, if possible to be scorched by its Fire, which was hidden so humbly in commonplace Bread and Wine. How often I had knelt there, frozen stiff and still wearing the stink and stain of the farmyard, "watching" anew the Lamb's holocaust, then avidly and thankfully eating His Body and His Blood.

A short while later, Brother Francis drove me out and left me at the top of Kopua Road, beside the main highway that runs between Napier and Palmerston North. We agreed to meet up sometime, some place, to pursue the revolution.

I hitchhiked back to Auckland that day.

The Abbot's Shoes

As my family stood singing the Psalms late in the morning during Terce-Sext, I picked up a ride over the Kaweka Ranges and north to Taupo. When they stumbled back to church, from their early afternoon siesta I was in a van, barrelling through the Waikato's lush dairying country. As evening came, the monks of Kopua, in single-file, again lifted their voices to the Saviour who is "not willing that any should perish".[1] I was standing beside one of Auckland City's main arteries and "rivers of steel", doubting at long last (but too late) the wisdom of my flight. The full extent of my folly hit home when I knocked on my unsuspecting parents' front door, at dinner time. That night my Trappist fathers sang together their usual haunting evening prayer: "Shield us Lord in our waking hours. Watch over us while we are asleep. That we may watch with Christ, and rest peacefully." I lay awake in the spare bedroom, listening to the city roaring nearby, and pondering my mother and father's demeanour over dinner; their expressions a mixture of pleasure, disappointment and anxiety.

I moved on to an old workmate's house, and

---

1. 2 Peter 3.9 (KJV)

crashed on a bare wooden floor. During the day I visited friends and prayed before the Bread of the Altar in churches. At night I became the "dog" of Proverbs; the fool repeating "his folly".[2] The imagery is apt. I doubt very much if Jonah the Prophet came up smelling sweet, lying on the beach after his whale ride had ended. And yet, here is the mystery of it all and the end of my days hidden away with Bernard's sons. It was not the whale that chose to heave the seer out and into a foreign land. It had been the Lord who "commanded the fish, and it vomited Jonah onto dry land".[3]

---

2. Proverbs 26.11
3. Jonah 2.10

31

'Tis Mystery

"'Tis mystery all!" wrote the 18th century Methodist hymn writer, Charles Wesley. The Apostle Paul considered a Christian life to be essentially mysterious, something sacred and hidden until it is uncovered by God Himself. "Listen," he wrote, "I tell you a mystery: We will not all sleep, but we will all be changed."[1]

The novelty of being back in Auckland, footloose and fancy free, wore thin quickly; my money ran out even more rapidly. Quite by chance and very mysteriously I ran into a man who had taught me at primary school. I went and lived in his base-

---

1. 1 Corinthians 15.51

ment, worked in his garden, fell in love with his daughter. She and I talked the sun down, and almost back up again; Jesus of Nazareth and changing the world, monasteries and communes, pacifism and prophets. I said to Penny, "I'm not going to leave Howick without you." We left six weeks later, married.

The story of my marriage to this beautiful, intelligent and Christ-like creature is not for these (or perhaps any) pages. On one of our later visits together to our Trappist family, Father Benedict took Penny aside to predict that, "God will use someone as little understood as Peter to renew His Church!" He then went on to explain to her that as with Mary, the Mother of our Lord, "a sword will pierce your soul too".[2]

Our journey together over the next thirty years or so appeared to put more and more distance between me and Kopua Road. But we never forgot the community. My memories of them peppered my conversations. They continued to profoundly influence me, as I navigated my peculiar way from Catholic journalist to Presbyterian preacher to itinerant Pentecostal revivalist. Although it did at times

2. Luke 2.35

become almost deathly faint, the pulse of the Hours of the life of the abbey was always heard and felt by me … in the depths. I was learning (sometimes with confusion and even anguish) that I could never go back to nor leave what I had run away from. The older I got, the more I recognised and experienced how thoroughly I had been not merely influenced, but shaped and marked by my very brief Cistercian apprenticeship. "Train a child in the way he should go," the Proverbs so succinctly expound, "and when he is old he will not turn from it."[3]

Most mysteriously I dreamed frequently and vividly that I was back in the monastery's enclosure. It was usually daytime, and I knew that I would have to leave by evening. I had the sense that the community knew I should not be there, but they tolerated my presence, knowing that I was just visiting. On one particular occasion I dreamed that Father Basil told me that he had never really understood just how completely serious I had been about wanting to be a monk. I woke up with a great sense of relief that any misunderstanding over

---

[3]. Proverbs 22.6

my intentions had been cleared up with someone I admired and owed so much.

On another occasion (as I slept) I found myself standing at the foot of the steps up to the abbey's High Altar. Father Basil helped me ascend, but when I got to the top I was panic-struck because I could not remember how to begin to celebrate Mass. This holy monk who had so modestly and graciously opened so many doors for me in 1971-72, stood beside me and quietly said, "I will help you to get started."

What did our Fathers intend when, in framing "The Apostles' Creed", they asserted that they believed in "the communion of the saints"? Well, many things I am sure. But among them, I trust, is the fact of the friendship that exists between Christians. And this includes Believers here and in Heaven too; and it is affection that effortlessly bridges the infinite and wafer-thin gulf between the two. The remarkable Carmelite prophetess Thérèse of Lisieux said that she was certain the citizens of Heaven looked after her and thought of her as their child.[4]

---

4. Thérèse (1873–97, France) wrote "Autobiography of a Saint", among "the greatest books of spirituality ever written".

'Tis Mystery

I later had good reason to recall the second dream, and Father Basil's promise to help me get started. Just two years after that "night vision" (in 2005), I crashed and burned; too much travelling, too many sermons, picking up and carrying too many burdens. I had always considered that prayer was absolutely indispensable and central to my life and ministry. But I was aghast to discover and to experience that my devotional practice was seriously meagre and dangerously rickety. It did not sustain me in a time of real tribulation, whose relentless waves exposed me and then my true foundations, to which I returned. I wrote away and purchased a Benedictine prayer book[5], and began, upon my knees, to inch cautiously back into the currents of God's contemplative stream.

---

5. "The Glenstal Book of Prayer" (John Garratt Publishing, 2001 Australia)

32

Great Preoccupation

I prayed a very simplified version of the Hours in the morning and evening for the next six years. At the same time I returned to the contemplative springs I had begun to drink from as a teenager. I read again Thomas Merton and Charles de Foucauld. And discovered Edith Stein and Raïssa Maritain.[1] All the while, like God's beloved Israel in the Wilderness, I sang and dug, dug and sang, "Spring up, O well!"[2]

---

1. Charles de Foucauld (1858–1916), a French hermit and "founder" of the Little Brothers and Sisters of Jesus. Edith Stein (1891–1942), a German Carmelite nun, philosopher and martyr. Raïssa Maritain (1883–1960), a French mystic and "lay" contemplative.
2. Numbers 21.17–18

Then during 2011 I wrote a series of essays[3] out of the burgeoning conviction that a Church that exists alienated and divorced from God's contemplative tradition and its own communitarian roots is at best disabled, at worst mutilated. It is doomed to quail and fail in the face of every Day of the Lord ... whether that be social catastrophe, the collapse of a civilisation, or the Second Advent.

Among the disciples of Jesus Christ there have always been those who are "wired", supremely passionate and concerned for what God is doing in local churches, or missions. But my controversy with both the Catholic and Protestant Churches is that they have "fenced off" the "gently flowing waters of Shiloah".[4] As divinely beautiful and powerful as the great monastic movements (Benedictines, Cistercians, Carthusians, Carmelites) undoubtedly are, they remain exclusive ... of married couples and families. And generally, Protestantism (with one or two notable exceptions) has obfuscated or denied the possibility of Jesus Christ ever calling any of His followers to "live to pray".

---

3. "The Tribulation Church" (RevivalStreams, NZ 2012). A serious call for the Church to become "the house of prayer" evoked by the Lord Jesus Christ in Matthew 21.13, and to return to our communitarian roots. www.thetribulationchurch.co.nz
4. Isaiah 8.6 John 9.7

Great Preoccupation

The Body of Christ in its entirety ought to make sincere, generous and wholehearted provision for anyone and everyone whose vocation and occupation is to pray. Denying an authentic call of God is to dishonour the Caller. To suppress a purehearted Christian's spirit is to "put out the Spirit's fire" and treat the prophetic "with contempt".[5] It is just sheer madness to ignore the God-given sources and founts of our strength, especially in the face of great tribulation.

The poet and mystic, Raïssa Maritain prophesied and cried out for this during her own ordinary, yet contemplative life. She absolutely believed that a life of prayer was not the preserve only of members of the great Orders like the Carthusians or Carmelites. In a certain sense she anticipated contemplation for the masses, not just a spiritual or religious elite. Her vision was that the "constant attention to the presence of Jesus" by the man in the street — "persons hidden to the world" — would be needed by the world "if it is not to perish".[6]

At the beginning of 2012 I felt that I needed to

---

5. 1 Thessalonians 5.19–20
6. "Raïssa's Journal" Ed. Jacques Maritain (Magi Books, Albany NY 1974)

radically and completely overturn my own interior and exterior worlds and try to live my message of "The Tribulation Church". I had to attempt to begin to learn how to "live to pray". It is difficult to imagine doing anything that is at once so simple and easy and yet so complex and difficult. It requires no effort really just to say to yourself, "My singing of the Psalms morning, noon and night, is now my occupation, my work." But then you catch yourself scuttling through your prayers, like a kiwi through the undergrowth, eager to get on with your life and the real responsibilities of the day. I doubt if I will ever completely win this battle. After all, some within the most venerable contemplative communities continue to feel pressured and debate the necessity of activism and productivity. But it will always be a noble and worthwhile conflict.

I honestly doubt I would have lived very long into my twenties had I not been received, "hidden" and nourished by my Trappist fathers within their sanctuary. God used them to build into my life those foundation stones I appeared to have little use for almost half of my life. But Providence exposed them through some trials and some light, and now,

Great Preoccupation

limping and diffident, I am trying to build a little upon them. I am dreaming of many tiny monasteries, "invisible" in urban and rural wildernesses, where young and old, married and single can together "live to pray". These houses of prayer are not going to be renowned or distinguished for their architecture, organisation, usefulness or output. They will be known for their willingness to labour tirelessly and endlessly in prayer, to be "together" and to have "everything (material and spiritual property) in common".[7] In the eyes of the world (and even many of God's own People) they will seem poor and feeble, unimpressive, unimportant, unprofitable. But in holy obscurity such will shape the sinews of history. They will generate little smoke or flame. But in their "world" where hearth and grate are trivialities, there will be heat. And it will be immensely fierce, completely invisible and utterly silent.

"The fire of the Lord fell and burned up the sacrifice, the wood, the stones and the soil, and also licked up the water in the trench."[8]

---

7. Acts 2.44
8. 1 Kings 18.38

33

The Smallest

"The kingdom of heaven is like a mustard seed, which a man took and planted in his field. Though it is the smallest of all your seeds, yet when it grows, it is the largest of garden plants and becomes a tree, so that the birds of the air come and perch in its branches."[1]

The house of prayer in which I now sit is only a few feet square. When my Southern Star family planted their monastery, they sang their Hours jammed together in a little bedroom in a small shearers' hut. At the end of every Psalm they nar-

---

1. Matthew 13.31–32

rowly avoided colliding as they bowed and sang their "Glorias".

The Psalms I sing are out of the book used by the Trappists of Genesee Abbey in upstate New York. It was handwritten "by one monk over a period of nearly a year". And so, three times every day I feel again the warm current of my kinship with the contemplatives of Kopua, La Trappe, Clairvaux. Most abbeys follow an order or schedule of designated Psalms for particular Offices on certain days. I am led by the "perpetual Psalter", which allows these holy songs to unfold in the successive order and plan determined by Another. Thus, I am in one sense cast adrift, but always on the ancient and irresistible draughts and tides of the River of prayer. Its depths have never been plumbed, its width cannot be spanned, and its power is infinite. Its purpose is to sweep all before it into Heaven; "to renew the face of the earth"[2], to turn Gehenna into Eden. Its canticles scald and heal the lips of their singers, leaving us crushed and ennobled, diminished and exalted. They have forever cycled down from Heaven through Tent, Temple, synagogue,

---

2. Psalm 104.30

The Smallest

monastery, church and prayer house, before being returned to Paradise.

Although I am by myself here, it is impossible to be alone. The most solitary Psalm singer is nevertheless part of an immense choir that enfolds and subsumes all who have ever and will ever tell and chant them. At every moment of every day there will be some, somewhere rendering up these everlasting songs of contrition, spiritual poverty and adoration.

I do not ever have a mathematical plan when I begin an Hour. I could never tell you how many Psalms I will sing. Why? Because I have the great need to just keep on singing until the programme is not the issue; until I feel that I'm no longer skimming along on top of the River, but have in some way or other become submerged. Perhaps the more one is "in" the water, the more we are abandoned and subject to its torrents and eddies.

And I gladly add to these Psalms the prayers others have already framed to sigh, sing or shout. It is not that I do not know how to speak out freely for myself. It matters very little to me the author's century, "tribe" or theology. I will claim and repeat (if needs be endlessly) any phrases that have already travelled here from the Throne and back again. I just do not very much care if they are the petitions of a sun-blackened Desert Mother, a levitating medieval stigmatic, a sober-sided Congregational theologian, or a Pentecostal revivalist.[3] I love them all. I love their prayers and I will constantly fill my mouth with their ancient, ever-new intercessions.

When I begin a time of prayer, I choose to make the "Sign of the Cross". But not because I am a ritualist or superstitious. I just never, ever want to forget that I have nothing in this life whatsoever to glory in or boast about except "the cross of our Lord Jesus Christ, through which the world has been crucified to me, and I to the world".[4] I deliberately make this gesture "largely", in an exaggerated way, so as to draw near to my companions in another of the River's streams … the enigmatic Carthusian hermits. I call to mind their ancient motto, "Stat crux dum volvitur orbis" … "Stands the Cross, still point of the turning world"![5] And as I am praying I want to remember how (in a

---

3. Mother Sarah, Catherine of Siena, P.T. Forsyth, Evan Roberts.
4. Galatians 6.14
5. Others translate this, "The Cross steady while the world is turning." I wonder also about, "The world revolves around the Cross"?

moment of Reformation madness) they were massacred upon the pavements of London just because they were so patently holy, and because they would take none but Jesus Himself to be their King and Head.

To love at a distance (of both time and geography) my older brothers and sisters is to be plaited and joined to them and who they are, what they do and stand for. Perhaps some sincere folk have carried the "communion of the saints" to unbiblical extremes. But it is infinitely more dangerous to simply turn our backs on this "great cloud of witnesses"[6] all around us. It is difficult to imagine these who have travelled ahead of us as stony-faced, aloof, passive. After all, the purpose of their watchfulness is to influence us to "throw off everything that hinders" in "the race marked out for us".[7]

I have no problem at all in asking the Lord for the intercession of such who now live in His presence, and with whom I feel empathy and closeness. I profoundly value and earnestly covet the prayers of the saints on earth, so why not those in Heaven? And so, in the centre of the prayer wall of this

---

6. Hebrews 12.1
7. Ibid.

house hangs a copy of a drawing of the Suffering Servant (seen in a vision) and sketched out by a leading light from another of the River's wonderful streams ... the Carmelites. While 16th century dynamos like John Calvin in northern Europe toiled as teachers to revolutionise Christ's Church, John of the Cross likewise laboured in Spain, but almost entirely upon his knees. I think it unlikely they would easily have recognised each other, but I am positive both were equally devout men, moved by the same Spirit and zeal for their "Father's house".[8] On the same wall are photographs of others who have "lived to pray" ... Thérèse of Lisieux, Charles de Foucauld, Edith Stein, Roger of Taizé. This will perhaps strike my Protestant companions as peculiar or unnecessary. It's too late for me to worry overly about the palatability or acceptability of this man's devotional life. I like to remember such friends for whom the life of prayer was everything, and who paid a high price to live it. And these pictures are not just windows through which I can remember them. I believe that by them they are able to watch over me, most likely with some

---

8. John 2.16–17

perplexity and discomfort, but always (I hope) kindly and prayerfully.

I do wonder if perhaps death cannot divide or scatter a contemplative community. I hope that they remain together in Heaven, as they once were "in this valley of tears". Do my brothers and fathers of Southern Star together now perpetually behold One whose head and hair are "white like wool, as white as snow", with eyes like "blazing fire"?[9] And do they still see those they once loved, and who loved them in return? I believe so. And I will continue to hope that Father Joseph is able to see with a little joy and satisfaction that this unruly and difficult runaway is now growing old upon his own knees, and that he still "wears" his Abbot's shoes.

---

9. Revelation 1.14

Glossary

Chapter room. The place for community decision-making.

Choir. That part of the church where the monks sing the Hours.

Cloister. Covered walkway inside the enclosure.

Enclosure. An area within the monastery where the monks live and which is off-limits to others.

Kiwi. A flightless, nocturnal bird, native to New Zealand.

Marae. Maori tribal meeting place.

Marists. The Society of Mary. An institute of priests created in France in the 1800s with a focus on education and missions.

Scriptorium. A monastery's library.

Tangi. A Maori funeral.

About the Author

Having worked as a newspaper and radio journalist, Peter Robertson embarked on a 35 year career in Christian ministry, involving parish, lecture hall and itinerant preaching. His "final quest" is for a contemplative life in which prayer is work and work is prayer. Other books he has written include *The Tribulation Church* and *A Great Sign*. Peter lives in New Zealand with his wife and family.

www.ingramcontent.com/pod-product-compliance
Lightning Source LLC
Chambersburg PA
CBHW051357290426
44108CB00015B/2056